"Driver, do you stop at the station?"

"No Madam, a train does that. This is a bus, it stops at bus stops."

Version 2.0

By

James Henry © 2012

Artwork by James Henry © 2012

GW00383531

Dedication

I'd like to thank my mother for having me
and my father for having my mother, thus creating me.

Foreword

The foreword is usually written by someone who knows the author well and extols his or her virtues. I thought it best to leave this blank.

Preface

This book started off as a blog. Stop rolling your eyes skyward, it was one of the popular ones - not one of those boring journals flooding the internet to limited interest audiences. I was 48, redundant, and had applied to be a bus driver. I decided to share my experiences both funny and sad, with you. I called it 'Driving a bus' because it was about driving a bus. With me so far?

There were two routes (pun not intended) I could take. One was the gritty real life exposé and the other, a causal relaxed look behind the scenes of the transport industry. I chose the latter because I wanted to keep my job, but there are still very good bits. I will take you through the interview with a manager a third of my age, an embarrassing medical and the joys of trying not to crash a 12 ton coach. Later, we meet the general public and all that brings. Enjoy five years worth of mayhem. Oh yes, it's not for children.

Special thanks to you, the general public, without whom this book would be blank pages. Colin Walton and Lloyd Bayley for their invaluable help and support. Also my wife Karen because I might get my leg over if she likes it.

I have changed some names to protect the guilty and to get out of having to pay people money.

Chapter One: Interview & medical

Every author knows it the first page that has to gain the readers interest. I'm not an author, but I know you will find this book both amusing and interesting as well as an invaluable insight in to something we take so for granted. Rather than dragging you kicking and screaming into my story, I thought I'd just give you a small sample of what's to come.

I'm starting to get the hang of this service now. It still has it's moments of course, last night I was coming back along an open stretch of road at 50mph when I got caught by a gust of wind - I almost had a trouser accident. I wondered how I would have explained that to the Control Office.

"Control here, Mick speaking."
"Hi Mick, Jimmy here, I've er . . . had a little accident."
"What's the damage?"
"It's a . . . spillage."
"Can you mop it up at all?"
"Not from where I'm sitting."
"Ha ha, you make it sound like you've shi . . . (Pause) oh."
"Yes . . . please, don't tell anyone."

It could have been a lot worse:

"Hi Control, Jimmy here."
"Hi Jimmy, what's the problem?"
"The bus fell over."

Shorter I think you'll agree, but the trouser accident could still be part of the scenario. Still, it didn't fall over and my pride remained intact, I just slowed down a bit and managed to polish the teeth marks out of the steering wheel later.

First steps towards becoming a bus driver: OK, bus driving wasn't exactly uppermost in my mind, in fact it hadn't even strolled past until I was behind one and saw the advert on the back - 'Become a bus driver, paid training.' ah, the magic word - 'paid'!

The interview took place in mid June. I had already been for a couple of interviews for jobs and had got on well. I didn't get those jobs obviously, otherwise this book would have had a different title. Previously, the only interview I had was 32 years ago - redundancy is a great leveller.

I applied and received the application forms. I filled in without using a crayon which I though would make a good first impression. I was surprised about a couple of questions, one being the use of drugs . . . should I be using them? It turns out not, apparently they do drug testing - I'd better stop drinking Night Nurse then. Application duly dispatched and processed, I received an invitation to attend an interview.

The interview was held at the town bus depot. I sat and waited in the front reception and watched as the public wandered in and out collecting bus guides, maps and asking the receptionist various questions. I was impressed with her knowledge; she could have been making it up for all I knew.

I had just finished reading the posters on the wall for the fourth time, when a door opened and I was beckoned in to the manager's office. I felt a sort of awkwardness being directed to 'Take a seat' by someone a third of my age. I resisted the urge to look for a school satchel under his desk. There were two chairs, one facing his desk and the other facing a filing cabinet. I chose the first, I think this was a test. "So why do you want to be a bus driver?" he asked. An obvious leading question and one I had prepared for. "I need the money." I replied.

Well that was the answer I wanted to give and impress him with my honesty, but we all know that it wouldn't tick any boxes. The standard "I've always wanted to be a bus driver ever since I was a boy" answer really didn't explain why I've spent 32 years avoiding it.

"I've always wanted to be a bus driver." I replied. "Ever since I was a little boy."

He seemed satisfied and proceeded to give a rough outline of what the job entailed, occasionally referencing his copy of the 'Boys Own Book of Buses'. I nodded in a professional manner when he paused and threw in the occasional "Yes I see." at other appropriate moments. This seemed to go down well.

He stood up and I did the same, making an assumption that the interview was over. I was just about to offer my hand for shaking when he said, "And now there's a short written test to complete."

Now this, I was totally unprepared for. Ok, not totally - I've been through the school system and could read and write, an example of which you are currently looking at, but didn't expect to be tested on it. I was taken to what was really a store room with a table and chair and handed a four page paper. "I'll come back in say, half an hour." he said. "Half an hour." I repeated, he did ask me to.

He left and closed the door. I don't know why, but I scanned the room for cameras.

Page one, a short statement of two paragraphs told of the ethos of driving a bus and customer care. This was followed by four questions whose answers were in the above text, it even said that.

Page two, a test of numeracy. 10 questions asking what the correct change should be using the given combinations of ticket prices. Very basic stuff, I'd been good at maths ever since I was eleventeen.

Page three, A little harder for me, the 24 hour clock. My watch only goes up to 12 and my fingers 10. If a bus leaves the depot at 08:02, reaches the end of the route at 10:03, waits 7 minutes then takes 33 minutes to return to the depot, what time would it arrive back? I got one wrong but one that others tripped over I got right, some redemption I felt.

Page four, this was perhaps the most fun and I got it wrong. I was faced with a comic strip cartoon showing four scenes that were continuous. My task was to explain what was depicted in each scene. How could I get it wrong you may wonder? Simple, I had explained it from a third person's point of view rather than that of the driver.

The whole thing had taken me 15 minutes including a reread; I started to wonder if I should start colouring it in. Time passed slowly, I was tucked away alone in the store room and eagerly listening for footsteps outside, it wouldn't do for the door to open discover me rummaging through their shelves now, would it?

I did pass with 80%, with a five minute talk afterwards, it was clear that I understood the questions but had just phrased it differently. He asked a couple of extra ones just to reassure himself I think.

One was of interest. What would I do if I was carrying two old ladies late at night and a drunk got on the bus, staggered passed me and sat down without paying? The drunk in this case was not loud or completely out of his tree, just the worse for wear. I answered that I would carry on until the other passengers had alighted. This apparently, was the correct answer. However since then I have learnt that there is much entertainment value to be had from a drunk on the bus . . . and the passengers love it.

My interviewer seemed pleased with the result. We chatted for a few moments and he then informed me that pending a medical, he would be pleased to accept me for further training. I walked out with a happy smile, were I younger I might have punched the air and whooped or something, but that might have upset my guide dog.

My wife was pleased to hear of my success and a small celebration would be in order. Her idea of a celebration was a huge plate of ham, egg and chips with a couple of beers. My idea was a shag.

In the couple of weeks I had to wait for the medical appointment, I filled my time with important research into the travel industry - or to be honest, looking for blogs that tell it how it really is - I can assure you they are startling in their honesty. I know, I wrote one.

This was my first ever medical and I found it worrying on two levels. Would the doctor find something wrong with me that I didn't know about and will he (or she) want to see my Willy?

I arrived in plenty of time for my appointment and parked up a short distance away. I do like to come early which frustrates my wife. I settled back to read a book to pass the time. It was a warm July morning and I wound the window down. This was the moment a passing seagull chose to crap on the shoulder of my freshly ironed shirt - for a brief moment I actually admired its accuracy.

Realisation soon set in - the shirt was ruined! I pondered with the idea of going back home but the chance of a clean ironed shirt waiting was doubtful. Instead, I did the only thing I could think of - I got out of the car, took off my shirt and sat back in. Having spent a good ten minutes scrubbing away with an old used tissue I found in the glove box, I managed to reduce the stain to an oily patch - better but still noticeable.

A new problem was approaching in the form of two policemen. I spotted them as they turned in to the road where I was parked. What would they think if they saw what might appear to be a naked man sat in a car at the side of the road, his hand moving vigorously up and down in short strokes? A dread thought rushed across my brain, I hoped I wasn't parked close to a school . . . that would take some explaining.

As luck would have it, they crossed the road and went off in a different direction - second disaster averted or so I thought. Time had marched on; I needed to walk the short distance to the surgery for my 9:30 appointment. I had been forewarned that a 'sample' would be required and I had saved up. I revealed myself to the receptionist - not literally, not my type. Disaster two was about to strike. "Ah" she said after a few seconds tapping away at an imaginary keyboard, "We have you down for 10:40, could you come back then?" she asked. "Yes of course," I replied, "Not a problem." I lied. I turned on my heels and took my sloshing bladder outside. It's when you can't go that it starts to nag and behind me a perfectly good toilet in the surgery started to call my name.

I now had an hour to kill and jogging was out of the question, as was standing by a waterfall. Perhaps I could wander in to the town and look for a second hand parrot shop - which would save me explaining the oily stain on the shirt at least. I also had a minor brain wave that would cure my pressing bladder problem, a condom.

It's at times like this that the most absurd ideas come to mind and seem reasonable, logical even. Why not just buy a condom and have a wee in it? I could then just tie it off and keep it in my underpants where it would remain at body temperature and then when sample time came, it would be on tap so to speak. You soon see the problems - how much does a condom actually hold? It is really designed for a much smaller volume. What if it breaks or I can't untie the knot? Worse still, what if I have to 'sample' in front of someone? Sadly, I dismissed the idea and returned to the surgery to be closer to the toilet just in case the dam burst.

The Doctors waiting room was crowded with the usual suspects and I busied myself reading a pamphlet on smoking whilst pregnant. I noted the obligatory Readers Digests scattered around with their pages fluffy with over thumbing. Time passed slowly.

I was eventually summonsed by a nurse and we proceeded to a small room. A few questions were asked. I was weighed, measured and counted (One) and then the plastic cup was presented - sample time. My first thoughts were one - it's too small and two, was I to do it there and then?

With only a woman's intuition and experience, she read my mind and said I was to sample 'mid flow' and it's just outside and to the left. Ever grateful I proceeded at a pace to toilet sanctuary.

In stark contrast to the rest of the building, the toilet was tiny and right next to the waiting room. Having positioned myself, I took care to try to aim at the side of the bowl and avoid the water. Nothing is worse than a whole room of people hearing you piss, everyone would hear me stop and restart again, and the old ladies next door would look at each other and mouth silently "mid flow sample."

Mission complete, I washed my hands in what must have been the tiniest hand basin I had ever seen. Disaster number three was to raise its ugly head. The combination of tiny basin, fast flow hot tap and light grey trousers were to prove my undoing. I had managed to splash my crutch area; a dark toilet accident patch appeared.

I exited the toilet with cup in one hand and my medical form held down at crutch level in the other.

Back in the relative safety of the nurse's room, I semi-gestured to my crutch and uttered "tiny sink you have there."

You always feel an explanation is required to alleviate guilt even if not guilty.

The nurse took the sample and removed the cap with practised ease and proceeded to dip in some sort of stick - this was the drugs test I was informed. After a short while, the all clear was given and I was sent back to the waiting room carefully covering my crutch area with my D1 PSV drivers medical form. I was so glad it was A4.

Without to much of a wait, I was directed to the doctor's office. I had no idea of what faced me. I assumed I would end up naked with an embarrassed smile trying to make small talk; I was wearing my superman Y fronts too. Disappointingly my trousers remained in place.

The medical was a simple one, normal health questions, some prodding and thumping with a hammer which I found very amusing - oh for musical knee caps. Next a sight test. A standard eye chart hung on the wall. I scanned it for rude words to but no avail. This was followed by testing my peripheral vision and my ability to stand on tip toes seemed to satisfy the doctor. I was fine, much to my relief. I had an element of doubt when he listened to my chest and made a second pass to assure he was hearing things right. This medical was to prove to my future employer that I was stable enough to drive a bus whilst standing up, semi-naked, gazing out of the side window, but the side benefit was to assure me that nothing strange was looming on the horizon.

Chapter two: Training day.

I now have a starting date. In a week's time, I would be a trainee bus driver reaping the benefits of free travel and a high visibility vest, all the rage I hear. I have received my provisional PSV license and I'm a learner again. The thought of driving a bus with 'L' plates on, I found highly amusing.

I would spend the Saturday down town buying a couple of pairs of smart trousers and shirts. My last job was a manual one where the dress code was casual, bordering on scruffy. Turning up for work wearing a T shirt proclaiming 'Same Shit Different Day' might be apt but not ideal, besides, I'd thrown all my old stuff away, marking the end of an era.

In the high street, I paid more attention to the buses than usual. Close up, they're bloody huge and what I'd not noticed before were the front wheels. They're not at the front, they're set back about seven foot from the front of the bus and about four foot behind the driver. What was the point of that I thought, I would find out later.

I had a message from a friend in Amity, Arkansas who used to work on the buses in Texas; I called him Charles because that's his name. He related a funny story to me that happened whilst he was there. The American buses were all equipped with a microphone for addressing the passengers and the drivers often complained that the flexible neck of these microphones, which were bolted to the dashboard and were far too short, but that was to change when a female driver had had enough and complained that every time she lent over to use the thing her one of her bosoms got caught in the steering wheel. That must have been a sight to behold and a good reason for me to slip in the word bosom.

Official confirmation arrives at last. 'Please arrive at 8:00 am for induction and bring with you your licence, two passport size photographs and a bus if you have one'. Bugger it, this means another trip down town to find one of those silly little photo booths that young people seem to mistake for brothels.

It had been a while since I last used one of these. I adjusted the seat, pulled the curtain across and read the instructions. Money duly inserted, I gazed lovingly at the mirrored screen ahead of me waiting for the flash . . . any moment now . . . or now . . . or . . .FLASH, one picture taken. I waited for the next, and waited and waited. No one had told me it takes just one picture and prints it four times had they. I had gone to the trouble of wearing a tie and had expected to pose four times, getting at least one picture right. Instead I had four badly framed passport size photographs with loads of space above my head and no collar and tie. I had planned on making the fourth picture a bit cheeky, well you have to don't you. I was wearing a thong too.

Arriving home, my wife had received a phone call, start time was now seven in the morning and the training takes place 80 miles away. I had taken some comfort that the training would be local, this was bad news.

Monday, D day: Arrived at the depot in plenty of time and was issued with my lovely Hi-Vis Vest which makes me crash proof - deep joy. I spot a group of people who, like me, looked lost and out of place, "Trainees?" I asked, they nodded. I had them at an advantage, for all they knew, I could have been the instructor; I resisted the temptation to start marching them around the bus depot yard.

A large plain coach was sat in the yard with its engine running, the front displays the sign 'Not in service' and the penny drops - this is the training bus. We clamber aboard assuming the guy in the drivers seat is the instructor. We were off to have our induction, wagons roll.

Two hours later we arrive at our destination, another bus depot. During the trip, we had all introduced ourselves and were on first name terms, having learnt each other's backgrounds and interests. No, total bollocks! Like all strangers lumped in some form of public transport, we said nothing to each other and just gazed out of the windows the whole trip.

It turned out the bloke giving the induction was on holiday. We found sanctuary leaning against a wall that had the most fag ends around it whilst the collective instructors grouped and occasionally peered at us and laughed.

It turned out that two of our group were on their second week and they ware given the task of reversing from one yellow box marked on the ground into another. The second box wasn't directly behind the first, that would have been too easy. Instead, it was offset forcing the driver to do a sort of 'S' shape backwards and they were using the coach we had driven up in. Box 'B', as it became known to protect its true identity, was surrounded with cones. They had three goes each, then changed over.

Wanting to sound intelligent, I asked the instructor why they were using a coach which was obviously much larger than a bus. He reasoned that if we could drive that, we could drive anything the company threw at us . . . cunning.

"Ok your turn." said the instructor. I looked at him blankly, then did the classic looking behind me bit - the other buggers had sidestepped, "You must be joking," I said, "have you seen the size of the bloody thing?" strangely, he had. "Go on, jump up, you might as well get a feel for it." he said smiling.

Suddenly, everything was different. The steps seemed higher, the interior Tardis like and worst of all, all eyes were on me. Bugger it, I'll have a go. My first mistake was not adjusting the seat. My attention was on the dash board, everything about driving had just dribbled out of my ear, and I was lost at the wheel of a 12 ton coach.

Pedals three, steering wheel one, hand brake, hmm, missing. I looked around and asked, "Where's the hand brake?" This is when I discovered the instructor wasn't on board. I had the singular company of the 'Reversing-a-bus-aimlessly-in-to-a-box' trainee. He pointed to a short black lever on the dashboard; he then offered some words of encouragement, "Try not to run over the instructor, he's driving you home." I think he smiled.

With the engine running, always a good start I feel, I reached out for the gear lever and it smacked me on the back of the hand, it was about three foot long and wiggling around like a pole dancer on acid (I imagined . . . my wife was never that obliging). After a brief game of 'Catch me if you can', I managed to force it in to reverse which involved leaning out of the seat and thrusting backwards with all my might. If I had adjusted the seat, it would have helped but you don't think of these things when you're crapping yourself, do you.

I gently released the clutch waiting for the bite, nothing happened. A small voice in my head said "Handbrake?" . . . it turned out not to be mine. I looked out of the windscreen at the rest of the guys who were busying themselves holding up a wall and they waved. "Your turn will come you bastards", I thought. Handbrake released, it started to roll backwards and I took up the play and applied some power.

Reversing a bus is like reversing a car with all the windows blacked out - totally blinkered! I had one hope . . . the mirror. Travelling at several feet per day, I somehow managed to line the bus up with box 'B' and with the occasional lean out of the window, I somehow lined up with the cones on my side. The others were totally obscured and probably under the coach making a dragging noise. Another problem now arose, how far back was far enough?

The coach, I later learned was 42 foot long; I imagined the 'B' box would have been 43 foot. Logic said, when the front of the bus drew level with the first cone I should stop. In reality, I had reversed in so slowly, I had to keep tapping the throttle to edge it in. Mission accomplished, I engaged the hand brake and was rewarded with a satisfying phutshssssssssh from somewhere below . . . it wasn't me.

I'm not a smug person, but I was pleased with myself. I had driven a bus for the first time. OK, backwards yes, but driven none the less. Thinking my turn was over and not wanting to steal the limelight, I motioned to get up.

"The instructor wants you to do an emergency stop." said box 'B' boy. "?" I replied.

"See that yellow line ahead? Drive up to that at 15 mph and hit the brakes without locking them up.", "And the building beyond it?" I motioned. "Don't hit it."

Having felt the power of the brakes, I knew I was in for a seat jolting time. Nonetheless it was to be done and amazingly . . . I did it. I didn't quite reach 15 mph nor did I brake on the line but a little before, however, my confidence was growing. I carried on doing this four more times before changing places with another trainee. Later on, I was to have another go and here is the point where I nearly brought the house down, literally.

Everything was fine - driving around the parked buses to line up in box 'A' no problem. Reversing back in to box B, well, I got there on several occasions. Not always straight but in the box at least. Starting the emergency stop, however, was to be my downfall.

The first error were the pedals For some unknown reason, my brain forgot which was which and I stalled the bus no less than four times before getting it right. Finally, composure regained, I set off for the 15 mph target speed . . . and hit the wrong pedal . . . nothing happened, it was the clutch, not the brake.

Why I used my left foot instead of my right is a complete mystery to me, but the coach proceeded in the direction of the building, the trainee behind me lunged forward to reach the hand brake, when I suddenly got it right and stopped a few feet from the brick wall of the building. The trainee was flung forward but had held on to a passenger support and came to no harm. I looked out at the instructor; he smiled and waved me on to have another go.

Chatting later with him, he was to tell me that making mistakes was all part learning curve and to carry on was vitally important, I tended to agree, it was working for me. I must have driven and reversed that bloody coach a dozen more times, literally completely on my own, me and 12 tons of steel, aluminium and possibly a puddle of wee wee under the drivers seat.

I came home, hot and bothered. Today has been one of the hottest days of the year and we had all felt it. I loved the unhurried pace that had been set - talk about giving a kid a new toy to play with. It was the most fun I'd had for ages without the help of a battery driven marital aid.

Day two: When we arrived, I was almost panting at the instructor, "Can we play now please, please, pretty please?", "Oh go on then." he replied and made a gesture of throwing a dog a bone.

This July turned out to be the hottest on record for many years. Our shirts stuck to our backs, sweat trickled between our cheeks, you know where I'm talking about don't you, go on, be honest. We spent about an hour playing, taking turns and actually helping each other out. We were starting to bond, in a team way, not holding hands or anything like that you understand, just because our shirts were wet and our nipples aroused, that was just coincidence, obviously.

There came a time for me to stop, fun as it was, a bus on a hot day is like a mobile green house. Despite all the windows being open, we didn't have the benefit of a breeze as we never got much above 20 mph in the confines of the yard. I took my self off for a tea break. The second day you got wise, handfuls of 20p's for the vending machine.

During a break, a break being defined as a time when everyone was in the same place at the same time, we were shown the Hazard perception Test. This was one of three tests we would have to pass. The idea is a simple one, a video taken from the point of view from a car windscreen showed a badly edited journey around a town, a village and a motorway. The 'Testee', a word I coined that sounds like a single testicle and always brought a smile, sat facing the screen with his hand clasped on a mouse. All you had to do, was click if you saw a potential hazard and click again if it should develop into a genuine one.

The triggers to look for were things like a car stopping at the side of the road (Potential hazard) and then the same car door opening, (Genuine hazard). The same applies to someone on the pavement approaching the road - are they going to cross, or change direction and walk away? . . . Simple stuff.

Problem is, everything becomes a hazard but you have to spot the ones the designer thinks you should spot. Cunningly, he had set hidden response time windows in place to catch out those that just click at everything. I had a go unofficially - my score was 50 out of 75, which turned out to be the minimum requirement. This was disappointing because we all think we're better than we really are. We blamed the mouse, of course.

I know I make it sound like we were having loads of fun and everything seemed lackadaisical, but as there were eight of us, six newbie's who each had to have half an hour reversing and doing emergency stops, and two who were more advanced that went out on the road with the instructors, leaving us to fend for ourselves. That, added to the four hours getting there and back, made for, dare I say it . . . a bus man's holiday.

Another day, another hand full of 20p's. Everything was much the same as yesterday and starting to get boring. Lots of milling around and leaning on walls was to be had by one and all. I got another go on the Hazard Perception test but this time there were serious problems. The computer we were using was old, and by old I mean the normal beige colour had changed to a yellow tinge. It also creaked as it warmed up, must be the valves, I guess the AE carved in to the side stood for Albert Einstein. We persevered with the glitchy video and scored a massive 13!

What was working was the theory test; this was another computer based exam. Now the theory for driving a bus was, in my eyes, stopping, picking up passengers and driving off. In the words of Jeremy Clarkson, 'How hard can it be?' Wrong, as usual.

This was the first time for me that I'd done anything like this. I had passed my car driving test when cars where still powered by coal, and as long as I didn't run over the man walking in front with the red flag, you passed.

We had a go anyway, after all, we were sensible car drivers and were bound to get most of the answers right. When I say 'we', I meant one person sat in the chair and we all gave our opinions to the questions shown, collectively we couldn't fail.

We failed. 24 out of 35, the pass mark was 30.

Each question had four or more answers to pick from. Some were intentionally funny and clearly wrong, others were phrased to sound sensible but were actually distractions from the real answers, whilst some had more than one answer. We then had goes as individuals; this would separate the men from the boys. We watched in silence as each took their turn, all secretly trying to memorise the answers but the questions kept changing and at the end you only saw the score not the answers, clever buggers. What we needed was a book with the answers in.

"Here's a book with the answers in." said an instructor handing each of us a copy.
"Are you allowed to do that?" I asked in my best innocent voice.
"Well how else are you going to learn? You've got a week to digest it."
"You mean we've got to eat the bloody thing as well?" I ducked his open hand as he swung for me playfully (I hope).
"Your test is next week, absorb."

Bugger, a week! I stopped myself doing a Clarksonism again. This book had 1000 questions and answers, was as thick as an old phone directory and we have to pass this or fail the whole course.

Day and night I looked at this book; I'd have to open it eventually.

If you want to find out what the test is really like, then why not try out a shortened version here at www.theory-tests.co.uk? I did, and discovered I could pass the car theory easily but worryingly failed the PSV (bus) version by three points, shame on me.

On the trip back home, we witnessed the aftermath of an accident involving a bus. There was what can only be described as a tear along 70% of the side of the bus, several shattered windows and a crowd of people. Folks love a good accident; suddenly their rush to get home seems less important if there's drama to be seen.

We were later to discover that the bus was going around a round-a-bout as normally as a bus can, when a foreign lorry driver not familiar with our traffic regulations, failed to give way and collided with the bus. No one was injured, thankfully.

The rest of the week passed in the usual fashion, Wednesday was followed by Thursday, Friday hid behind Thursday until the appropriate time then popped into place, then the weekend jumped in, bless it.

Chapter Three: Air fresheners and theory test.

The weekend was a welcome relief, no more getting up at five thirty in the morning, the chance of a lay-in and some rumpy pumpy if I was a good boy. Everyone wanted to know what it was like driving a bus, I had to admit that I'd not even got out of the depot yet, but I had a book to read, how exciting was that?

OK, time to lighten the mood with something that made that weekend more memorable. I got molested, twice in fact, by a household utensil, one of those times sexually, knew you'd be interested.

My wife has a fetish. Now before anyone gets over excited I should explain it is centred on air fresheners. Strange I know, but let me try to spread more light on the subject.

'Darling' as she is affectionately known, (I'm terrible with names) started out just the same as everyone else, purchasing a plastic air freshener, small and unobtrusive. Its design was such that you just pulled the cover off to reveal a green gel with the odour of some passing flower and I wouldn't be surprised if pine cones were involved somewhere.

I thought she was happy enough but no, she wanted bigger and better. What was to follow were the glass ornament air fresheners, simple glass tablet style things, again with a gel backing - half the gel for twice the price, for a while she was again, satisfied.

Time passed and I started to notice a change, a new device had hit the scene - this one plugged in the mains supply draining our electricity. The 'thing' resembled an over sized plug with a small glass tube which, when heated, gave of a gentle odour. Hmm thought I, now she's taken to hiding these things in unused plug sockets about the house, very High Tech.

Time passed yet again (it rarely goes the other way) and low and behold, a couple of months later, yet another object was to appear, or should I say, take over from the last. The company who made the last device had come up with an upgrade, now it came with a tiny fan to disperse an oily aroma of pine forests and wooded glades. Now these did get on my nerves because they hummed slightly, just at the right wave length to annoy me.

One day there was silence, the sound had disappeared, I said nothing. After a while, I began to notice a new odour. I thought I knew them all, but this one was much stronger for a while, in fact the smell came and went. Further investigation revealed the Godzilla of the air freshener world, a 11" tall monolith of a device, hewn from the very core of the earth (yes, plastic). This contraption was admittedly very clever. At set times, it would spurt out a measured amount of freshness (smell disguiser), it's source being a spray can, it's power was derived from a battery.

Not having given it too much thought at the time, I carried on with life until one day I noticed this thing had a flashing green light on the front, I was surprised I had not noticed it before. I approached the machine which had been placed at head level and then . . . psst, a face full of freshener spray, yes, the light was a warning that it was going to fire and it had to do it whilst I was full face on.

The second assault was to happen some time later, the same sort of device was involved for it had spawned offspring. The new 'death spay' was positioned in the bathroom on a window sill, it's nozzle of death aiming directly at the shower. This was to be the most effective attack about my person. Having just showered and dried but still standing facing the shower, I bent down to pick up a dropped bottle of shampoo when this thing attacked, it's jet of cold 'fruits of the forest' targeting where the sun don't shine.

There is nothing that can describe that feeling (I'm sure Oscar Wilde must have said) and so I'm not going to, I'll leave that to your imagination, but don't probe too deeply.

Back to work, week two: We had all been complaining how the days were starting to drag on without actually achieving anything real. We said this to each other of course, not out loud, heaven forbid someone should hear us, but the instructors knew, apparently they were saying the same thing but in a different voice. It turned out that the normal compliment on the training bus was four, not eight, all this was about to change.

One chap failed to turn up and two more advanced drivers were taking their tests this week. Yes, we had started calling ourselves drivers, what next, badges perhaps! We were now to get more involved - this meant we went on the road, not driving, that would be silly, we were observers, watching what the two advanced drivers did, listening to the instructors . . . instructing.

And there's more - we were getting a new coach. OK, not exactly new, in fact it looked identical to the tatty heap we'd been playing with but this one was an automatic! Goody, one less pedal.

Now I'm not stupid, please don't vote on that, I do know the difference between an automatic and a stick shift, I was just confused why we had to change just as we were getting the hang of it. The kindly faced instructor informed us that all modern buses were automatics and therefore we had to learn to drive these said automatics but the two 'Advanced drivers' came from a depot where they still had a couple of stick shifts that weren't due for replacement of a few months to come, hence they had to complete their test on the old coach, we, he assured us, were getting the better side of the deal.

The two guys had two intense days of driving, we watched, studied our theory books and generally kept out of the way, if these guys passed, we all moved up a notch, we would literally be sitting nearer the drivers seat.

The big day came, we sat grouped together in the yard pretending not to look as each of the two candidates waited to be called by the Department of Transport Test examiner. Each entered the coach for five minutes, both came out with the examiner closely behind, one left the yard the other slowly walked around the bus with the examiner pointing out things, perhaps the examiner hadn't seen a coach before, I wondered. Once circled, the trainee got back inside and started the engine, on a signal by the examiner, he rolled the bus back from box 'A' perfectly into box 'B'. All the time the examiner, clipboard in hand watched oh so carefully, changing position, marking his board. Next the brake test, we all wondered if the examiner would get inside for this one, of course not, he positioned himself beside a sturdy metal bollard, this guy's no fool . . . spoilsport.

Brake test successfully passed we assumed, it looked good to us, and we're experts now, they drove off out of the yard and into the real world. I tried to think of something witty to say. I turned to the instructor, "Not invited then? I asked. "Not allowed." he answered, paused and then said, "Shall we play with that over there?" he pointed to a double-decker bus.

Who's a big boy then: Dave, we called him Delightful Dave, was one of the more talkative instructors, a guy who's so laid back the back of his head touches his heels. He was going to let us play with the big toys.

Oh boy, Oh boy, Oh boy, big bus. The other guys were getting used to me now and were more than happy to have me volunteer to be the first to try things. We clambered on-board like a scene from the classic Cliff Richard film Summer Holiday, but my hair was nicer.

"OK Jimmy, you can do what you boys usually do." said Dave
"But I haven't got any tissues," I retorted, "You know what I mean." he replied, killing my next line about coming on a bus, stone dead.

Now a 'Decker', as they were known in the trade, looks like a cumbersome machine, as aerodynamic as a brick, as tall as a house and as wide as . . . well a bus. Despite this, they are an absolute joy to drive - smooth, responsive and a little bit majestic, not unlike my wife. It was slightly akin perhaps to sailing a galleon on a calm tropical sea, the breeze in your hair, the sound of distant coconuts, grass skirts being mown, scurvy pustules popping. I was in my own little heaven, so much easier than that battered coach we'd been calling home; this thing had spunk as our American cousins disgustingly like saying.

We learnt later that day that Rodney, not Dave was to be our instructor for the rest of the course. We were to be split up. Dave took three guys and Rodney the other three, I was in the 'other' three, and our play days may be coming to an end.

Rodney, who we later christened 'Rod the Rod', had different a style. He had not actually instructed us as yet, that will be coming very soon, but I have paid attention to what he has said to other trainee's and comments to me for the future. Rod's style is more factual and a little sarcastic but in a friendly way, such as "It would have been good to indicate there before we kill someone." However, if he felt the trainee was getting a little narked, then he would immediately lighten the situation. Two very different styles but both work, and they both impart pearls of wisdom; after all, they actually want you to pass.

Our theory test had been moved forward, the induction we should have had on the first day was now tomorrow, a bit like closing the stable door after the horse had bolted, still, a day in a classroom with slides and a film show was like being back at school, should I wear shorts and bring some crayons I thought.

We were still playing when the training coach returned. We had become so engrossed we almost didn't notice it drive into the yard, we stopped to allow it to pass knowing the irony it would cause if we forced the trainee to slam on the brakes when he had thought he had reached the relative safety of the depot. The test didn't end until the coach was parked and the engine was off Dave informed us.

It was so obvious that it was almost embarrassing. We stopped, they parked up, we stayed stopped watching across the yard for a clue, our faces pressed against the windows trying to look nonchalant, hard to do when your dribbling. The trainee had got out of the driving seat and was sat on the ledge inside, in front of the windscreen, his back towards us. There was much gesturing from the examiner and nodding from the trainee. Eventually, the trainee slowly put one arm behind his back and did the thumbs up signal - he'd passed. The decker rocked and cheered, the examiner glanced over towards us, word travelled fast around here.

One down one to go, more time to kill. I am starting to hear the amusing stories that every job has and look forward to repeating them here as they arrive. Rod and Dave were talking about the double deckers and how hard they are to tip over, apparently they have to lean at over 37 degrees before the point of balance is broken, then it falls over. I love a challenge.

Unknown to the common people, the likes of you and me, a decker is fitted with a primitive computer system that stops it falling over, sort of. It balances out the air bags that support the suspension. Test it for yourself next time, get everyone to rush over to one side and you'll see it balance out, so disappointing I know, perhaps one day you'll catch it off guard.

It is a point of amusement for the instructors when on the odd occasion they use a decker to see the driver physically lean in to a corner as one would on a motorcycle even though the bus remains upright. They also have a bit of a passion for low bridges, the instructors that is, they will know an area well and purposely direct you down a road with a seemingly low bridge, they know it will fit, they will even tell the driver to "Just go for it." but the driver will still instinctively duck his head, I know, I still do. Oh, the second trainee, he passed.

Induction day: After the usual two hour journey, it was time for the company to formally introduce itself to us. This was the usual thing; a spokesman would give a talk about the company. How it developed, where it is now that sort of thing. Nothing that couldn't have been written on the back of a dirty postcard.

Most of the drivers have little interest, as long as they are paid at the end of the week, that's fine. I however, do like to have some background knowledge and managed to look as if I was interested, scoring brownie points hopefully.

Something that did surprise me, other than finding out one of the lads was wearing tights, was that bus companies get fined for being early, yes really. You'd think people would be happy wouldn't you, but if it says a bus should be at a bus stop at a certain time and comes early, a problem I know well, it mustn't leave until the advertised time. On the other hand, if it's late, tough titty.

Tomorrow is my theory test day and so tonight I'm really swotting up and not just looking at the pictures. The good news is that it's going to be held in the local home depot.

Tomorrow never comes - this one did: Today was theory test day. Arrived as usual and was directed to a Portacabin behind the bus shed that I didn't even know existed. Here lived a couple of computers to practice on. What I hadn't realised, was that it was a two part test, the theory test included the Hazard perception test. I had convinced my self they were two separate tests - they didn't tell me they were only separated by three minutes.

The three of us had two hours to practice. Hmm, two computers three trainees, was this a sign of things to come? hope so. I love a disaster, it livens up the day. I went for a wander while the other two played the mock test. I found myself in the engineering department and I tried to look like I was meant to be there, yes everyone else was wearing bright orange overalls but I had a Hi Vis vest, I think that trumps it. I spotted a door marked toilet and headed that way; if you have purpose, people don't ask questions and you blend in.

Strolling out pretending I'd just dried my hands, I spotted our coach. It was having fresh Gaffa tape applied, must be an upgrade then.

I returned to the Portacabin with supplies - cans of Coke and a copy of Nuns Monthly and settled down for a play, on the computer that is. I did well, today would be my day.

No, it turns out it wouldn't, the real test computer is locked away in an office somewhere and refused to link up with head office, no connection, no go. Four and a half hours they tried, bugger.

"We'll have to do it at the training depot, I'm afraid," said Rod. "Good thing they've put Go Faster Gaffa tape on the training bus then." I answered. "Good god, we're not going now, I'll miss my dinner." he replied. We looked at each other; it was easier than trying to look at yourself.

"Go home and..." the rest of his sentence was never discovered, there was no one there to hear it.

The next day was more of the same. Our coach had developed a fault and hadn't been fixed, so the morning was spent swotting - flies mostly, can't complain really, we're getting paid for this, I mused. We had a little bit of light relief late morning; we opened a window without asking.

The afternoon was different, the coach was fixed but it was too late to travel anywhere far and so we were taken out to the edge of town and shot, sorry wrong story. We were allowed to drive on a real road around a housing estate. As always, I volunteered myself, it's not because I'm particularly brave, I just like to get it out of the way so I can relax and watch everyone else.

The circuit was left, left, left and left. Amazingly, it brought us back to where we started, odd that. Part of the route did involve a dual carriageway with a 50mph limit, seeing we've never got above 20mph, it could be trouser wetting time.

I closed the doors, the others had wisely elected to get off and wait on a nearby bench which meant they could smoke and fart without distracting the driver or pissing off Rod the Rod. I pressed the 'D' button for drive, pressed the foot brake down, took off the hand brake, mirrored, signalled and pulled out - easy peasy. Driving a bus or coach is simple, two pedals, one for go the other for stop, the hard bit was turning. In the yard, there were no kerbs, cars, people or dead dogs. Here in front of me, was the real world and it was moving toward me.

The first challenge was a roundabout, but as we were taking the first exit there was no problem, or so I thought. There was a bump from the back end, "That'll be the back wheels running over the pavement." said Rod. I checked the mirror, he was right of course. Next roundabout, same again, "Snap" said Rod, "Bugger" said I. Now the dual carriageway got up to 45 mph before I started to think about stopping, there was another roundabout, this time I watched the nearside mirror as I turned. The front wheels on the bus go round and round, they were also several feet behind me. The back wheels don't follow the same line as the front ones, the sneaky buggers try to take a short cut. The answer is to turn the steering late, you actually overshoot where you would normally turn, then turn. Because you have taken the corner wide the front of the bus was going to go over the traffic island. "Keep turning" said Rod, I missed the bollard and waited for the bus to mount the island kerb, it didn't happen. "Well done, don't forget to straighten up." added Rod.

The last turn was also a roundabout, I used the same technique as the last one and just scraped the side of the rear wheel along the kerb edge, the other trainees on the bench just saw the bus come round the corner normally, Rod said nothing, he didn't need to. It took me a while to work out what was happening. It was all down to the front wheels not being at the front, this means the bus has an overhang of about seven feet.

This overhang glides gracefully over the kerb with a clearance height of about six inches. If the wheels were at the front, it wouldn't go round corners at all.

The next trainee did exactly the same. On the last turn coming in to our view, the back wheels mounted the kerb - shamefully I tutted, bloody amateur. We probably had about five or six goes each and learned a lot, Rod had told us how important it was on the approach to a turn to take up the whole road if necessary to prevent a car trying to come up the inside. As the coach turns the gap between it and the corners narrows, the car would be forced on to the pavement, its better to block it and stop it. We wanted to play some more, but it was time to head home. How pleased I would be to be able to tell my wife that I could now turn left.

Test day up north: Finally I got to take my theory and hazard perception test, all that could be heard on the two hour journey was the turning of pages from our study book, supplemented with the occasional scream.

It was about 11.30 when I was summoned to attend my theory test. I entered the room and the test examiner was present. I do know that he's not a man to be influenced, not that the gun in my trouser waist band was loaded.

Anyway, I have digressed; it was just him and me in the room. I sign a form confirming my driving documents. Legal requirements complete, he asks some seemingly odd questions such as, do I have any audio playing devices on my person, any paper, books, pens, scratch-pads or listening devices and such like. It would appear that some people try to cheat, it would require a full body tattoo to get the 1000 questions written out and you can bet the answer you want is on your arse.

I found it amusing but understood completely. My name is entered onto a computer and I am placed in front of it, a brief explanation and I'm on my way, the examiner leaves the room.

Part one of the test is a selection of 35 random questions taken from the 'Official DSA theory test' book, all these are multi-choice and generally common sense prevails. What I was dreading, were any technical questions. A couple did arise but I knew the answers. I did have one known problem, and that was how long a break the driver has to take after 4.5 hours driving, I didn't have a clue, the option 'early retirement' wasn't one of the listed answers.

Part two was the Hazard Perception. After completing the first test, there is a 3 minute break then you click the 'next' button. A short instructional video explains what's expected. Moving on and we're away. I think there were 15 clips of various driving scenes, and I had to click when I saw a possible problem, such as, a pedestrian walking near the road edge, or a definite one, like a car ahead pulling out in to the road. The later would cause the driver to either change course or speed.

It had been a very hot day, the room was stuffy, I was nervous, conditions not exactly relaxing, two other trainees ahead of me had passed, the pressure was on. I had the feeling I had failed about half way through, should I carry on and finish the test or just tell the examiner that I'm just not ready?

I decided to complete the test, might as well see where I was falling down. I pressed the 'finish button' expecting the score to appear on the screen, it doesn't. The examiner enters the room, presses a button on the printer and out pops two sheets of paper . . . the results. I remained staring at the now blank screen "Well done . . . You've passed." he said.

We all know how difficult it can be pretending not to be surprised when you are, you just can't help bloody smiling. "34 out of 35 on the Theory test" said the man from the ministry, "and 57% for the Visual Hazard Perception," he finished. We had sex and I left. (Not really, but I did leave the room).

Wow, almost 100% on the theory test! I was chuffed, bet it was the required rest break question that let me down; I had one chance in four of getting that right. The Hazard Perception result was disappointing, the pass is 50%, I'd scored enough but having doubts halfway through probably cost me the better result.

Still, not to worry, I had a certificate, I would spend the rest of the day trying not to crease it, after all, this could end up with another big plate of ham, egg and chips again, know what I mean?

Chapter four: Hit the road Jack.

Friday afternoon was to be my first 'Just-get-on-with-it-and-stop-snivelling' day. As you progress through the course, there comes a time when you are let loose to drive the coach in stages, to and from the training depot. My stage was from the depot to the motorway and then on to a truck stop halfway, to change drivers. On occasions, we'd stay and have a cuppa and chips – the staple diet of bus drivers, I believe. However it was Poets Day* and I was happy to forego the opportunity for a more experienced driver - beside, there might be some right-hand corners.

*Poets Day: Piss Off Early, Tomorrow's Saturday.

Week three, it gets almost exciting: We have two trainees from another depot who are having their driving test at the end of the week and they need our coach and instructor. This leaves the three of us at a loose end but not for long. We are to be transferred for a couple of days, to an instructor and coach from a neighbouring county. I hope he speaks southern. The bad news, it's a stick shift.

Now this is weird, the coach has a selection of gears and they've been thoughtfully numbered by the manufacturer, but it would appear that they have put first gear off to the side. I helpfully point this out to the temporary instructor, - his name his wife probably knows but I can't remember.

"We only use first if the coach is loaded, just ignore it and start in second." he informed us. "OK, I'll give that a go, also," I paused, "we've only driven on a proper road for an hour last week.", "Yes, I've been warned." he replied. "Good" said I, "It's the left hand side we drive on isn't it?", "I've been warned about you too." He smiled.

A passing airfield would be a good place to start, instead he found 11 miles of almost straight road in the countryside, he didn't tell me about the huge dips and hills did he?

The hardest thing was keeping the bus away from the edge of the road. Being 8 foot wide, I only had about a foot to play with . . . well almost, no one told the trees did they? I'll swear the bloody things leaned in when they saw me coming.

It took quite a time to get used to this, especially as cars and lorries came towards me on the other side of the road and I had to keep my position, whereas, it would be normal in a car to just move in just a touch. To make things worse were the mirrors, you have to keep looking in them, both left and right to keep the bus position correct - amongst other uses. My head was working loose.

I was slowly getting used to it, when around a shallow corner, appeared a tractor. Not a problem you may think . . . it was the combine harvester behind it that was problematic. It took three quarters of the road, thankfully he saw the words 'Driver Training' on the bus and pulled over for ME, bless him! I resisted going "Ow Ah" in my best west country accent. Well, I survived that and got to the end of the road, and the instructor made me turn around and go back, bastard. Not really, I was really enjoying it.

What did take me by surprise was what he did next. Having completed the second lap, he directed me a bit further, around a couple of roundabouts, down a slip road and suddenly I was on the M3 - bloody hell! I ended up driving down to the coast on the motorway. Talk about "in at the deep end!" Oh yes, didn't realise that a coach with 'L' plates could use the motorways. As long as you hold a full car licence and a provisional PSV, you're OK. This meant I could scare the crap out of car drivers as I passed by closing one eye nearest them, thus giving the impression I was asleep at the wheel. The blindfold gag may have been taking it a bit too far.

One thing I do find great with the instructors, is that if things are going OK, they don't say anything - small errors are overlooked. I clipped the curb once and just received a "hmm." I knew, he knew, that was enough. On one later occasion, I heard snoring - but that's best left unmentioned.

Both the guys taking their tests failed, sadly to say. One had 15 minor faults, 12 being the limit. The other just had two but were major ones which were instant fails. A minor fault for example, can be something as simple as the examiners back coming away from the back of the seat under breaking. In his eyes, this is harsh braking and is a no-no. Hate to be his wife!

The other guy's two faults had really annoyed us as they weren't really his fault to begin with. Being pig ugly, thankfully, wasn't one of them. This guy was perhaps one of the least nervous people I had seen. I cover mine up with bravado, he didn't need to, he was a cool dude.

Both the faults were the same thing but in different places, the culprits were roundabouts. As you approach a roundabout, you must be prepared to stop and wait for a suitable gap, then when clear, join the roundabout. It is vitally important that you do not cause any car to slow down or change course.

We'll call the guy involved John. That's not his real name, I wouldn't want Peter seeing his name in print, that wouldn't do. John approached the roundabout perfectly, right lane, indicating, the whole works. The roundabout itself was covered in large bushes, restricting vision despite the elevated drivers position. He waited for a clear moment, and waited and waited - it came. He accelerated out, when a car suddenly appeared at a speed not suitable for a roundabout and braked sharply. Peter sorry, John had no option but to carry on and that was his first fail.

The very next roundabout, similar in design, was approached in the same careful manner, again a clear gap came - again he accelerated in to it, a car, joined in from a road to the coaches' right hand side and unbelievably crossed lanes to the centre and shot across the front of the coach sounding its horn, this too was a fail. To be fair to John, it is unlikely the examiner was in a position to see this car join the roundabout and was only aware as it crossed the front of the coach, blind-spots affect examiners too, but a car had sounded its horn and that was enough.

Trainee one, he who's name wasn't John or even Peter come to that, had the opportunity to retake his test a week later but we never saw him again. Perhaps the embarrassment was too much, or he'd found a proper job, who knows, but John did a retest and passed with just six faults - half the maximum permitted.

"OK, who's driving us home then Jimmy?" asked Rod the

instructor. Bugger, he hadn't even paused between 'then' and 'Jimmy'. This would be the first time I would be on the road on the right bus with the right instructor, quite a revelation I felt.

Luckily the training depot is only a couple of roundabouts away from the motorway and so an hour's motorway driving was the order of the day. Now most of my travelling up and down or 'Observation' as I call it, was very much limited to looking out the right-hand passenger window due to my seating position but now being placed in the drivers seat meant I had to engage my brain and actually look where I was going and I didn't have a clue. I'd have to start reading the road signs; we are talking pre satnav here.

The instructors however, do make things quite clear with their directions, "take the third exit from the roundabout for the motorway Jimmy" this made it much easier to get on and just drive. On the whole, I was quiet pleased with my efforts. I did have a few moments here and there, a car ahead had it's front tyre burst but made it to the hard shoulder without affecting me too much, a container lorry came by and I expected the vacuum effect to take hold and the bus to be sucked toward it, but it was very slight and easily controlled.

One thing I never realised and I learnt a week ago is that all lorries are fitted with speed limiters preventing then from going faster than 60 miles an hour (as do buses). I now have a greater understanding of why it takes ages for one lorry to overtake another on the motorway and why when overtaken, you should allow space for the lorry to pull in when clear.

Do I drive my car any differently now I'm getting more experience on the road? The answer is yes, very much so. Road observation changes, road position and spacing come into play. Pulling in to bus-stops gets embarrassing.

I've been getting a bit more hands-on experience . . . and driving a bus too: Week four and strolling into my home depot first thing in the morning, a familiar sight greeted me - new recruits. A guy and a girl looking slightly lost, wearing Hi Vis vests that still showed the creases of recently being unfolded. It's a strange feeling, like looking back in time; I knew what they were thinking and how they felt. Just as I was closing in on them, Rod stuck his head out of the office door - I do wish he'd open it first.

"Could you get the training bus out of the garage for me Jimmy?" he asked. "The good one or the bad one?" I enquired. "Which ever has the most wheels today." he answered, keeping a professional straight face.

Ever-willing to oblige, I sauntered off garage-wise. Rod has a sense of humour, he can do quick wit or in this case he's decided to let it develop, he knew that when I came out of the garage in a bloody great coach the trainees would be shitting themselves and found it very funny.

This week, I would be finding myself (there I am, your turn to hide), more frequently in the driving seat, to and from the training depot, valuable experience of course. Had the odd cock-up here and there, notice how I resisted making a joke about cock-up, I must be maturing. Its really down to bad driving habits, hogging the centre lane on the motor way, not using the mirror enough, shagging the instructors daughter, sorry, couldn't resist slipping that in, well that's what I told him.

I noted with interest, that the new trainees sat mid way up the coach, something we had at first done, its one of those social things, I knew over time they would work their way to the front, I mean, that's where the fun happens.

The very front seats were reserved for the instructor and his lunch, sorry, briefcase with important documents in, mostly cheese. On the way, we picked up the Ministry test examiner, this was to become a regular event, it made driving more stressful especially as he sat directly behind me. No more scratching the testicles at 60mph, I thought.

A lady trainee from another area would to be taking her test that afternoon; it was to be her third attempt. Normally you only get two chances and you're out, but in very rare and exceptional circumstances, the examiner will permit a third. It had nothing to do with breast size. He has to be convinced that if he weren't present, she would pass; she would have had to have shown that it was the tension of the test and not her driving skills that were the underlying cause.

I spent some time chatting to her, trying perhaps to be a calming influence and getting her to relax – impossible, I know.

The moment her name was called, I could see her physically tighten up. I actually wanted to help, it must be true, I wasn't physically attracted to her! I don't think I was alone. As she got in the coach, as one, we all left the yard and went indoors.

In what passed for a tea room upstairs, I noted a couple of real bus drivers having a break and chatting casually. I think this involves putting on slippers and a cardigan. They were talking about lost property, apparently two bags of cement powder had been found abandoned on a bus last week. These things weigh 25 kilos each, not really something you could forget, I would have thought.

One driver offered the explanation that the owner had purchased said items at a DIY store that had a bus stop outside, however once on the bus, he realised that his final destination was some distance from where he was getting off. Now the maximum load for a person to carry is 25kgs, which is why these stores limit the bag size. It would take a strong man to carry two of these, one under each arm I would imagine, and the now ex-owner realised this and thought, 'bugger it, they can stay on the bus'.

"Why didn't he just take one then?" the other driver asked. His mate reasoned that the bus driver at the time would notice a man getting on with two bags of cement. He would also notice that person getting off with two bags, but he might also notice if there was only one and call him back. So, getting off with nothing was oddly less noticeable. The other driver looked puzzled for a moment as the idea slowly sank in.

"What happened to the cement then?" he asked eventually. "Lost property." replied his mate. "So it's still there then, the cement?", "Nope, had to get rid of, we can't store anything that's perishable." he answered. "Cement powder doesn't go off! "It does if you take it home and add sand and water to it." I laughed out loud; he looked at me, smiled and winked. I think I might like this job.

An hour and five minutes had passed and we all filtered downstairs and into the yard. The lady driver should be back and parked up and we'd know the result at last. She wasn't there, neither was the coach. I had a vision of it teetering on the edge of some ravine like the final scene from the Italian Job, the examiner prone on the floor pleading with her to move up the other end of the coach, sorry, have I given away the ending? Hate that.

She turned up ten minutes later, still sat in the driving seat, a good sign. After a very short pause, she got off the coach with the broadest grin I'd ever seen, she'd passed. I was so pleased, I didn't even look at her breasts.

One of the two new trainees from my home depot that I mentioned earlier, whom I shall refer to as 'Category D', is an ex-con, the clue is in his title. We didn't know this at first; it came to light the next day when we picked him from outside the open prison or bail hostel, as they are now known.

It is quite normal for selected prisoners to be allowed to work in the community, as part of their rehabilitation and those there are not the scary ones, I should add. There are a few murderers but these are more 'crimes of passion' rather than for gain or revenge. Mr. D, I should hasten to add, is not one of these and it's not fair to say why he is there but he is.

Today, I had a chance to have a bit of a chat with him and learned just how difficult it is for him to be able to get a job. He's honest and up front about it all and is very keen to get a 'proper job' and sort his life out and he has my respect for that. Mind you, he could be a confidence trickster!

Mr D was originally jailed in Wormwood Scrubs for quite a time but was transferred in to the open prison service a couple of years ago. This particular prison had a reputation of inmates just walking out. Mr D explained that those people are the ones with very short sentences, often as little as three months and so they don't have a lot to lose if caught. Whereas the wiser ones with the longer terms, just follow the system and reap what benefits that can be found and bide their time. After all, they have rent-free accommodation and the chance of a wage, why screw it up?

The weekend arrives and my wife leaves me. It's not all bad, she's actually taken the children away for a long weekend on the Isle of Wright, something we had planned and paid for last year before I lost my job. I unfortunately, had to stay behind. I was a working man now, but I have the house to myself. Did I mention dressing up in the wife's underwear at all?

Frustratingly, being alone can be counter-productive, I've got no one to show off to, but by the same token, no expectations to live up to either. I can leave the toilet seat up, pass wind in any room, put a fork in with the knives and no reaction, most peculiar.

What I did do, was eat kippers - love 'em, the smell lingered for ages and the house was incredibly quiet. No radio, no tinny Ipod music from the girls and bed time meant a whole double bed to myself, though I still found myself sleeping on the edge as usual. I did, and I have to admit this is something I really enjoy, set the alarm for 5.30 am just for the satisfaction of turning it off and going back to sleep.

Monday morning and the training coach is in the dock, not literally, it wouldn't float. It's in the garage having some extra rust added to replace that that fell off, and we had two more trainees but these were different, they were proper bus drivers.

Anyone who joins the company that was or used to be a bus driver, has to be assessed by the instructor to make sure they reach our exacting standards. Walking upright is a good sign, having both eyes facing forward is another winner as would supporting a certain football team endear them socially, oh yes, if they can drive a bus, it could prove helpful. It was this they were to do today, just for one day, in fact just an hours drive each but we didn't have a training coach did we?

"We'll take a bus" said Rod. "Don't you think the driver might get a little upset?" I replied, "Not a service bus you silly boy, one of the spares." he smiled.

Now this was annoying, we'd been training on a bloody great coach and only touched a real bus in the training yard and now, the one time we get a real one, some bloody ex-drivers get to play with it and to add insult to injury, I had to direct them. This entailed me standing next to the cab for 25 miles to the nearest large depot trying to hold on to the support, swaying like a drunken sailor tossing on a yacht, do sailors still do that? Dirty buggers.

Oh I do like to be beside the seaside: The next day, and the coach had been repaired and we were off for a jolly jaunt to a well-known seaside resort that had cliffs, not cliffs as in a lot of men named Clifford, cliffs as in big white chalky things holding back the sea, Vera Lynn liked them apparently and got quite vocal about it.

The day was spent driving round and about, no one knew the area except Rod the instructor which made each turn in the road something new and like all old established sea side resorts, the roads were narrow, busy and littered with people with knotted hankies and plastic union jacks made in China, the country not the pottery.

The return journey was down to little old me. Rather than go back via the main coast road as we arrived, Rob was to send me via the 'B' roads, which considering my little experience, was probably a wise choice. It was an area that it turned out, needed attention.

I have this nasty habit . . . it used to belong to a monk. Sorry, my other nasty habit was driving far too close to parked vehicles, it might have been something to do with having to sit at the front of the bus with the white line in the middle of the road going directly under where I was sitting. It can be a little disconcerting and I try to put a gap between it and me, after all, I would be the one killed first.

Missing the change in speed limits was another problem. Rod likes to see you rigorously using the mirrors and he will look for your head to do a sweep, right, forward, left, forward. This has to be done every few seconds and it's here that I miss the speed limits and checking the speedometer.

I also got caught out doing the right speed. A bend was approaching and the speed limit was 40, now that works for cars but not for a 42 foot coach, especially if a bloody great truck is coming the other way. Trucks you may have noticed, have huge mirrors sticking out, these are set at the same height as those on a coach. Our mirrors gently touched, which might not be the right adjective, perhaps 'crashed violently' would have been more apt. My mirror deflected inwards making contact with the drivers side window, I leant in to my left hunching my shoulders up and briefly closing my eyes waiting for the shower of broken glass. It didn't happen. I avoided looking at Rod in the rear view mirror and waited for the words.

There's nothing worse than being told off, well yes there is, not being told off, it builds tension. Rod didn't say a word, I pulled in to a bus stop, pushed the mirror back in to place and set off again, all totally wordlessly.

We pulled in to the yard at our home base, parked up and turned off. It was home time and everyone collected their bags and filtered off the coach slowly, far too slowly, they were waiting for Rod to let rip and didn't want to miss a syllable.

I had to get out of the driving seat and pass him to fetch my bag that was further down the coach; I just turned around to face him instead.

He held my gaze for a few tense moments, and then burst into laughter. "We've all done it, consider it a lesson learnt." said Rod. "I thought you might dismiss me" I answered. "It won't happen a second time, will it?" he said still smiling. "Nope." was all I had left to say. Bastard, he was good.

I do find that Rob can be a little contradictory at times, asking me the speed limit and why I'm not doing it then in the debriefing telling us that we should drive at the speed we feel comfortable at. On the whole, although Rob can be a little caustic at times, his aim is to make us bus drivers, and ones that he would feel were safe on the road. The past week and a bit, has seen a lot more driving taking place, when I pass (note WHEN), I shall miss the people who I am getting to know and the relaxed no-hurry days, but I'll not miss the training depot at all.

They say it's a bad workman that blames his tools: Driving back to the training depot the next day, it was pissing down with rain, the mesmerising swish of the wiper blades and gentle patter of rain on the roof proved too much for me . . . I fell asleep. Luckily, I wasn't driving the coach.

Both training coaches were starting to have major problems. Dave's had a head leak, put water in it and it just leaked out underneath. It was the first time I had seen underneath a coach, apart from the engine, which was mid-way there was stacks of room under there - no wonder illegal immigrants chose coaches, it's the only way to travel.

Our coach was just old and held together with Gaffa tape and painted-rust, but now one of the air suspension bags had developed a leak, turn it off and the whole thing starts listing to the left, rev it up for a couple of minutes and it rights itself, a great source of amusement at the moment. Both instructors were keen for them to fall apart. We've been encouraged to pick off any rust scabs we see, in the hope of creating a hole.

One bonus, was that we had to stop at a truck stop on the way back. Now truck stops won't be found along the motorways of Britain, they are usually tucked away, often on industrial estates. These aren't places for cars, oh no, it's for trucks and large drivers, not fat ones, although most of them are, but drivers of large vehicles.

Tattoos are almost obligatory as are checked shirts. The facilities are basic but functional - a shower block, a lounge, fuel pumps and café inevitably decked out in pine cladding inside and out. Here for a quid, you get a huge plate of chips - don't ask for an all-day breakfast, it'll take you all day.

You do get the feeling that you belong to an elite sort of club, the privileged few whose tea mugs hold a pint and their wallets are on a chain. We were, to some extent, the odd ones out. Trousers, shirts and ties but we were accepted, the poor cousin of the truck fraternity perhaps but on a par with Eddie Stobart drivers. I wondered what they might be thinking as we left the café and approached the coach that seemed to be leaning over allowing us to reach the normally high first step, the marvels of modern technology perhaps.

It's August and the sixth week of training: Sorry to say we lost 'Category D', he got caught shop-lifting and as they say, 'Go directly to Jail, do not pass go, do not collect your PSV.' Pity, he was a nice chap. He did give us a laugh a couple of days before he was banged up. He was doing some motorway driving whilst we all chatted away, when his mobile phone rang; he reached in to his pocket, opened the phone and told the caller he couldn't talk now he was driving. We just sat there in stony (not that sort of stoned) silence. Our collective mouths were gaping in disbelief. Rod obviously couldn't let that go and asked him what he thought he was doing and was he aware that it was an offence that can cost him his PSV if he was caught. 'Category D' just said "That's why I told them I was busy."

The August bank holiday was here, that's three days off for trainees, nice but frustrating. My redundancy money from my last job had run out a while ago and we were watching every penny. This meant not being able to take the kids out over the holiday weekend. I did feel a certain amount of guilt but by the third pint, it had gone.

When I pass my test (see how positive I am about this), I can look forward to driving a decent bus rather the bloody great coach we have at the moment. It always seemed to have a problem, it started leaking out of the air-powered door control, making opening the door a sluggish operation. It was going in to engineering on Friday evening and so we may not even see it on Tuesday when we go back, fingers crossed.

One of the questions I'm often asked is, "Where were you on the night of the . . ." Oops not that one, the other one. "How hard is it to drive a bus?" and the answer is, "anyone can." and it's true, it's going around corners that's a bit tricky. Narrow lanes comes a close second and parking is a bitch.

There are occasions when I find myself holding my breath; In a car its easy to weave in and out with a sort of harmony to oncoming traffic but with a bus we have to remember that the back end swings in and out like a model on a catwalk but with much less grace. It has been known for established bus drivers to pull out and knock down a bus shelter with the back-end wiggle.

Chapter five: Just say no or nothing.

Yes, I failed my driving test, Yes I kept it a secret, yes I have a thing about rubber but that's not connected, no I wasn't wearing my Captain Marvel big-bulge latex underwear. I was tempted not to mention it at all - the driving test, not the rubber. No-one likes being a failure, it's embarrassing.

Tuesday morning had arrived, as it often does, just after Monday. I had been asked if I would be willing to take a driving test at short notice, the original driver having shat himself, sorry, not turned up. The test was booked, the man from the Ministry was there and my underwear was clean. I said yes, I could have said no but that involved using different letters of the alphabet.

Rod took me out on the road for a sort of warm up and pep-talk, he was honest enough to say that the odds were against me, I didn't have enough small road experience and that if I failed, it wouldn't be a surprise or a disappointment, I just wasn't ready.

I used to be one of those people who like many of us, would start to build up the tension in advance. You know the sort of thing, you perhaps have a big interview ahead of you or have been summonsed to see the boss at 9am the next morning. You spend time in front of a mirror at home trying to rehearse what you're going to say. As I got older I didn't bother, I just went in thinking 'Just do it'. If only I'd patented that phrase, that would have pissed of 'Nike' the sportswear manufacturer.

Rod had warned me that the route the examiner would use wasn't one of the many we used in training. In fact, the instructors didn't know the test routes at all, they had made guesses from what past trainees had said and knew the five major problem areas around the town and ensured we crossed them at some time. It's here my experience was lacking. I was reassured that the test would only involve two or three of these hazards.

I buggered up the first one. We left the depot and went directly on to a 50mph road, the man from the Ministry who I'll just refer to as 'Hitler' at the moment, would expect each driver to go up to the speed limit and not play safe at 45. No problems there until he told me to invade Poland or take the first slip road coming up. This I knew, lead to a difficult junction with fast traffic approaching from my right. It also involved a tight turn that had to be taken slowly, due to a Keep-Right bollard. The technique was to go in a straight line over the junction and then at the right time, turn. I turned just a fraction, OK a couple of feet too late; the front of the coach wouldn't clear the bollard without knocking it down.

I was stuck across a junction! Fast moving traffic stopped moving fast, in fact they stopped completely, there was a coach in the way with 'L' plates on and a possibly red-faced examiner in a Hi Vis vest standing behind directing the coach driver, me, backwards. Sorted out, we moved off and he told me to pull in to the first bus stop or lay-by we meet.

It was an instant fail, if it had been a normal, shorter bus it wouldn't have been a problem.

The examiner, told me to relax, gather myself together and carry on when I was ready, I knew I had failed but the test must be completed. After this I was a wreck, nothing seemed to go right and I resigned myself to the task in hand in a more relaxed manner.

The test takes about an hour and then we returned to the depot and parked up, the examiner told me I had failed and that he need not tell me why as I knew only too well, I had actually caused him to stop a test and get out of the coach. However, he then informed me that if that had not had happened, I would have   passed!

After a short talk, I was handed the error sheet. Now you are allowed up 14 faults as long as they are minor and most people passed with anything from seven to twelve faults, my sheet had only five. My pass had I received it, would have been a good one. After that, I renamed him Hess.

I was taken aback a little by the reception I got from my result, normally a fail on the first test would result in a bollocking from the instructor, this didn't happen. Instead, I received understanding, which I found to be very supportive. Even Rod said I must have given him a good ride to score that low. We ended up laughing about my stupid error, accepted that it was down to my inexperience and that was that. I was grateful to have the experience of being on test, next time won't be so hard and I'm going pay someone to knock that bollard down. Don't ask me when my next test is, I won't tell you.

I knew today would be different. Rod, our instructor, was having a day off and we have Dave who's a lovely chap, always joking and smiling and so easy to get on with. The first inkling that something was up was when he appeared with what I can only describe as a mobile antique.

This was in the form of a 1960's open-top double Decker bus. It emerged that the mechanics had nothing to do and so in their wisdom, decided to fix the training bus and promptly removed the back axle which makes braking difficult - hence the mobile antique. Fortunately, we only had to take it to the next big depot 25 miles away and swap it for their training bus.

Dave was to drive this bus and we were grateful for that It had a crash gear box and involved something called double de-clutching. The cab was separate from the passengers, isolated and something like the classic Route master buses of old London, as iconic as a red phone box, except it was green. This model was called a 'Queen Mary' not because it was dead or had a passion for burning Protestants at the stake. Actually, I never did find out why it had that strange name, technically it was a PD3 which tended to send bus-spotters into public toilets with a box of tissues, bless 'em, they're harmless.

The seats inside were bench-style which meant your thighs rubbed against the person sitting next to you, the fabric was reminiscent of your grandmothers carpet, brown, old and covered in stains, the floor covering was equally dull lino and on the back of the seats were ashtrays. This was something straight out of 'On The Buses' with Reg Varney. Sadly, I knew who Reg Varney was. On the upside there was nothing actually.

The engine was tractor-like in both sound and motion, it shook, it rattled and it rolled. We, the masses, decided as it was open-top we'd be better off on the top deck and so at 8am on an unusually chilly morning travelling down the motorway at nearly 50, a group of obviously disillusioned trainee bus drivers played hide and seek with passing traffic.

We arrived surprisingly intact and in good spirits, but the flames of our passion were soon doused when we heard the other training bus had a faulty exhaust. All was not lost, there was a 25 seater mini bus that needed to go up to a bus station near our training depot and we could all jump on that, so we did, because it was there. We arrived an hour and a half later, only to find that there was nothing that could take us up to where we needed to be, we were stuck even further from home.

Bus stations are different to depots, you may have noticed, for instance, that there's more letters in the name and it starts with the letter B. This bus station was on one side of a large shopping centre and very busy, there were at least 12 bus bays and they were constantly on the move, the buses, not the bays, that would be silly. Dave, the font-of-all-knowledge directed us to a plain-looking door on the outside labelled 'Private'. I love going in to peoples privates.

The stairs led up to a cafeteria, not a public one, this was just for bus drivers and it was huge. There were two main rooms, one for stuffing grub down your gullet and the other for 'resting' drivers.

Of course, everyone was in uniform and we stuck out like the proverbial sore thumb in our plain shirts and ties and so we approached the counter with reservation. We were out of place here.

"Yes luv?" asked the lady behind the counter. "Sausage, egg and chips please." said I hesitantly. "New trainee?" she asked, taking a clean plate "Yes, how did you know?" I replied, giving my best quizzical and relieved look. "It's written on your Hi-Vis vest." she replied. It's amazing how the bleeding obvious can escape you.

We sat and enjoyed a heavily-discounted lunch, £2.50 was a bargain and I know in the shopping centre downstairs, people would be paying something like £6.99 for the same thing.

From where we sat, we could see the other drivers in the rest area. This consisted of an arrangement of sofas around the edges and a snooker table in the middle.

Most of the drivers were relaxing - the type of relaxing that involved setting an alarm time on their mobile phones, laying it on their chests and closing their eyes. Those that didn't have mobiles just used a piece of paper with a time written on it, relying on a fellow driver to wake them up.

I looked back from this scene to a driver who sat down at our table; he looked at me then to the rest area, smiled and said, "Yes, we do swap the papers over."

Having filled our collective bellies, we headed downstairs for a look around - we had fifteen minutes to kill and headed into the shopping centre. It was one of those really big covered ones with fountains, escalators and multiple exits. I got lost.

Panic started to set in after a while, this place had so many exits it would take me half an hour to find the right one and I only had five minutes to spare. Luckily, I saw another trainee leaving an Ann Summers shop and followed him as he took stuff out of the carrier bag and stuffed it in to his back pack depositing the empty bag in a bin. I joined the rest outside holding the Ann Summer bag. "What did you buy in Ann Summers then?" one asked me as I approached. "Just a carrier bag," I replied, it was obviously empty, "I have a thing about plastic bags." I winked at him. "Oh" he said and they all looked away.

The real purchaser however, was still looking at me. I reached in to the bag and pulled out the till receipt. He snatched it from my grasp, screwed it up and dropped it in a nearby rubbish bin. Pity, if he'd have looked at it, he would have seen it was for a sandwich I had bought yesterday. From this point on, he always seemed at-hand when I needed a 20p coin for the company vending machines, and insisted it was 'on him'. It's always intrigued me, the power you can have over someone by not doing something. The funny thing is, I didn't have a clue what he had bought but I wasn't going to tell him that, was I?

Dave, the instructor, joined us and imparted the news that we can't get to the training depot and that ironically we'd have to take the mini bus we arrived in, back to the first depot along with a mechanic from here that would then drive it back here empty.

All in all, a typical British farce in action. Still, it filled our day, perhaps one day it might be made in to a musical in the West End.

That evening when I arrived home, I found an email from an on-line bus publication, I'd been mentioned, my blog had become public. I had become famous for several seconds with bus-spotters. Not sure that's a good thing but people started reading it and commenting, they actually liked it.

I'd had a few emails in the past, most thanking me for the insights, some real drivers saying how well they related to my stories and another asking if I needed to improve the size of my penis. The internet is a wonderful thing.

Over the past few days, I have had the pleasure of being the 'first drive' of the day, I was far more confident. I drove a coach knowing exactly how long it was, how wide it was and its place in the space-time continuum. I put that bit in because some bus-spotters and blog readers are bound to be Star Trek fans and besides, it's one of the few words that have two U's next to each other.

I did have one problem on one of the mornings, I had pulled in to a bus station to collect the test examiner as normal and on leaving, you get in to a special bus lane who's only exit is controlled by its very own traffic light. Here I waited for it to turn green - a popular choice with many motorists except the very young.

It turned green, I accelerated and suddenly nothing happened, but it happened suddenly, the coach engine was doing at least 30 but the body remained stationary as did we. I'm sure this has happened to us all; we perhaps put the gear shift in to neutral and forget. The engine races and your face changes to red just as the traffic light does in front of you.

I checked the gear button, I checked the hand brake, I checked my underwear - nothing, there was no reason not to proceed and I was turning red - had I done anything silly? Two instructors and a test examiner sitting behind me didn't help, nor did the buses that were now queuing up behind me, please don't sound your horn guys. Honk honk, went the horns, bastards. "Check the air pressure Jimmy" said Rod "Ah." said I, "needles in the red, no air." this means of course, the brakes won't release. "Just rev the bollocks off it." came the technical advice. "Revving the bollocks off it now sir." I replied.

It took two phases of the traffic lights before enough pressure was gained to release the brakes and under instruction, proceeded to the nearest roundabout and returned to the engineering yard behind the bus depot. Time for the men in orange to work their magic.

Time passed numerically, the mechanic slid out from under the bus and looked up at me. Why did he look at me? . . . because I was the only one there, everyone else had gone off to the vending machine and my new 'Ann Summers' friend was getting mine, bless him.

"Sticky valve." said the mechanic pulling off his blue rubber gloves. "Well sometimes a trickle escapes if I don't shake it properly." I replied. "The air cylinder underneath I meant", "Oh that, thanks" I smiled.

Later that day, another more joyous moment was to arrive in the form of an idiot. On route we reach one of those very large roundabouts whose main exit is on the right, each lane on the approach is carefully marked in large white letters along with road signs proclaiming 'Get in lane'. As we rounded the roundabout a car appeared on the inside of the bus and stayed alongside as we went round. Indicating right for the exit the car realised he'd be crushed and braked sounding his horns in a slightly peeved fashion.

I carried on as everyone cheered. The car driver didn't enter the spirit of the thing and swerved past us on the right, pulled in front and slowed down to a crawl eventually stopping.

"Hazard lights on Jimmy, and don't say anything funny." said Rod. "Who me?"
"What the f*** do you think your f****** doing, you shouldn't be driving a f****** coach, you're a f****** menace pushing me off the road like that, I could been f****** killed, you're a w*****! "   " I replied.
The beauty of not answering back is that the antagoniser lost momentum, by now he was on the first step of the bus, a couple of my fellow trainee's had moved up ready for a bit of a discussion. "Well?" said the man.

"May I introduce you to the three gentlemen sitting directly behind me, Rod and Dave, they're driving instructors and the gentleman in the jacket is a test examiner from the Ministry of

Transport." Like the three wise monkeys they smiled down at him.

"I'm sure they would be only too happy to tell you about which lane you need to use and the dotted lines and arrows in those lanes." I finished smugly. His mouth opened and I'm sure some more asterisks were about to fall out when Rod said:

"Would you like me to phone the police for you, I'm sure they'd be very interested in what you have to say and perhaps might even like to see what was recorded on the coaches cameras?" said Rod. Adding, "And six statements confirming your actions."

"F****** w******" he replied and got off the coach and back in to his car. I closed the door.

"Nicely handled Jimmy, shame it's not part of the test procedure, you'd get a gold star." said Rod. "Drive carefully, I don't think this is over yet." he added.

It wasn't. The car driver sat there for a minute before moving off very slowly, we followed suit. This man, despite being in the wrong, decided to be a pain for as long as possible by dawdling along as slow as possible in front of the coach, causing traffic to build up behind.

He did eventually leave at the next major junction, I sure he was really eager to get to his counselling session.

This week was test week, it also means the two trainees that had joined at the same time I did were going first. I had taken one test and so had to go to the back of the queue. Very nervous and to their own minds inexperienced despite six weeks of training, both passed. I of course congratulated them, neither had had the time I had driving but they managed it. My test will be my last attempt - if I fail, I'm out of a job.

I would not, however, have missed this fantastic chance to drive around in a great big bus, it's not exactly a boyhood dream, we all wanted to be train drivers, a job I would consider easier - no steering wheel for a start. I had never seen myself as a bus driver, it's a job, it pays a wage, but I do enjoy driving. If I fail, I shall take it well, I'll be as disappointed as hell, but that's fate. If I fail to make the grade, I must accept the consequences. Don't expect too much from me for the next few days, my mind (and guts) are in turmoil, I have never been this

bloody nervous before except when I saw a jar of Vaseline in
the doctors office.

Chapter six: A license to thrill.

I passed; you probably knew that, considering I'm writing a book about being a bus driver.

It is incredibly difficult to explain just what emotions and stress I was going through that morning, it was my last chance and if I failed, I was out of a job. I do have a confession to make; this was not my second test but my third. Yes I lied to you, will you ever forgive me? Of course you will and you've been with me all the way, unless you've just flipped open to this page randomly.

Test two took place on Monday. I kept quiet about it as this is always advised; I was to be the second person of three. At the last minute, the first driver backed out and asked me to go first. This increased the tension but it was a case of 'Let's get it over with'.

I screwed it up on the reversing. As I drew out of the first marked box, no problems, got my angle about right, spotted the foremost cone in the mirror. I carried on reversing, I didn't turn in early enough, causing the rear end to touch a cone. The examiner walking alongside the open door asked me to stop - automatic fail. I looked up at the audience in the distance and heads were bowed, I felt not just my disappointment but theirs also. We proceeded with the rest of the test, which is normal.

On the return to the depot, the bad news was broken to me, but I knew anyway. The irony is that the drive around for an hour had been a good one. This time, I would have had five faults if I had not cocked it up - a very respectable score, zero has only happened once, from what I understand.

After failing test two, my instructor told me that the examiner was surprised I had failed, after all, he knew my driving well. I had been complimented on it more that once, I had tackled narrow roads, morning traffic, motorway accidents, pouring rain, stupid drivers and much more, In fact, I quite liked the small challenges put in my path.

In certain circumstances, exceptions are made. Normally two tests and that's it, but if a trainee has the ability to be able to drive to a set standard but fails purely because of nerves, then a third test is arranged after a gap of at least three days minimum. I think because my driving in the past had been to this standard and that I was perhaps the 'right' type of person for the job, this last chance was offered. My final test was on Friday and at least that would give me the week to feel sorry for myself.

There would be two of us taking the test. Me and someone called Mickey, that's not his real name of course, that was Michael. I didn't know him well but as we both found ourselves in the same boat, why there was a boat in the yard I never found out, We sought each others company - a problem shared is a problem doubled, I say.

On arrival, we had about 15 minutes to practice our reversing, we both had this weak point.

As Mickey started his reverse, I went alongside, reassuring him he was doing OK - He found this helpful. As Mickey parked in the end box and vacated the driving seat for me, he was called over to see the examiner in a parked bus to give him his documents, ready for the test. I carried on, took the bus to the start position, and did a near-perfect reverse in to the box, something I have done many times; I could just not do it with the examiner watching me. As I parked up, Mickey came over and ask me to present my documents to the examiner for inspection. We did the paperwork; he then said that I would not need to do the reverse test as he had been watching me all the time, a huge lump of pressure just fell off.

Mickey climbed aboard the coach, he was first out, so I left the yard and went inside. I knew that people watching adds pressure. Inside the building, I waited for a couple of minutes, pulling off the buttons on the vending machine and swapping them around whilst Mickey did his reversing bit and left the yard. When I came out, he was still there, still reversing. He must have stopped mid way and repositioned, that'll cost him a point.

Next, he did the controlled stop - no problem. The examiner started walking away, as that part of the test was over. Mickey had been told to just reverse the coach straight back in to the 'B' box, as I only had to do the emergency brake test, having passed my reversing test earlier. Mickey reversed over a cone and flattened it, not a good example but no harm was done, it had no effect on his test but he didn't know that.

My turn - no problem stopping the coach. I had to reverse it back out of the way but stopped short of the 'B' box, we only had so many cones. Next was the walk round. I strode around the bus with the examiner, pointing out required items such as where the emergency stop button was, water filler cap, fire extinguisher, hay for the horses, emergency exits which included the small skylights on the roof in case the bus fell over. We both knew the script, he nodded and I was sent to go get Mickey.

Mickey was now to take the second section of the test on the road for an hour. We had time to kill and the instructor needed some fags and this month's copy of Spanker's Delight. We jumped on the spare coach and drove into the town. I was doing the driving and I didn't give it a second thought, I just drove in a normal relaxed manner I didn't think the instructor corrected me once, I was comfortable - the calm before the storm perhaps.

We got back10 minutes before Mickey was due to return and parked up. He came in on time and circled the yard, pulling up next to us. The engine stopped, the examiner chatted away and we were trying to guess if he had passed or not. The examiner took an age waving his hands about, pen wagging, opening and closing his folder, but in the end we saw Mickey take out his driving license and pass it over, he had passed. Now it was my turn.

Yes, that time had come; I hoped that was adrenalin running down the inside of my leg. I was summonsed over to the examiners coach and sat in the driver's seat; this might be the last time. The examiner explained what was to happen, how he would direct me, what he was looking for and was there anything I wanted to say. I told him I was comfortable and asked if he took £20 notes? He told me to proceed when I was ready and to take a right out of the yard.

I selected 'Drive', checked my mirrors and blind spot, slipped off the hand brake and let the bus start to roll, remembering that there's a 10 mph limit out of the yard. My first obstacle was a right turn on to the main road. The road has to be totally clear for this manoeuvre but about 200 hundred yards up the road is a hill, it's a road going over a railway line and cars can just suddenly appear as if from no-where. As long as I had started my manoeuvre on a clear road, then it would be fine . . . It was.

We approached the first roundabout and If he said take the first left, I would be OK. This leads to an easy route with only a couple of obstacles. Instead, he said take the third road to the right, this led to town and the junction I failed on my first test attempt - my heart sank. Onward we travelled, took that fatal turn towards the junction and then he asked me to change lanes and turn right, taking us away from that deadly corner. He knew, he bloody well did that on purpose, I'll say this for the examiner, he had a sense of humour, I am pretty sure of that.

Now the pressure had eased somewhat, I started to relax. Next came the bus stops, I would be required to stop at three stops, pull in and get the bus parallel with the road, so I could eliminate a rearward blind spot. I had to make sure the gap between the door and the curb was no more than six inches, or twice the examiners penis length and not hit the shelter with the mirror. Pulling away involves checking your blind-spot, mirror checking, signalling and not dragging the shelter with you as you leave.

The next couple of roads were ordinary except that there was a change of speed limit from 30 to 40. It is important that you try to get to these speeds to show that you have read the signs, going too slowly gets a 'Failing to proceed' fault.

We were now in an area I did not know. The instructors take us all over the area, trying to cover every eventuality, guessing the test routes and the examiner can change it mid-drive if he felt so inclined. One road was just a mess of 'pinch points', which act as traffic-calmers. How it works the curb comes out into the road on each side, making a narrow lane in the very centre. There must have been six of these, at least. The secret is, to line up early and slow down a bit. Getting the front through is not difficult, it's getting the back to follow and not changing course until it has that proves difficult.

Now came a real test, in the form of a double mini roundabout but this was no ordinary double mini roundabout, oh no, this one had a traffic island in-between just to tease. The approach had to be made at less than walking-speed and involved 'aiming' the coach at a post until the front was almost touching the opposite kerb and then turning sharply, still at walking speed and 'aiming' at the traffic island. This ensured the back end came around and didn't hit the kerb. Next was getting the front overhang to overhang the traffic island until the front wheel was just about to touch the island's kerb and then sharply turn in the opposite direction. This brought the coach in to a straight line, ready to tackle the second roundabout.

The second roundabout was easy but it catches drivers out because they think the worst is over and get sloppy. Before you know it, the rear of the coach is going over the slightly-raised roundabout.

I didn't get cocky but kept the same speed all the way through. I'd done this before thankfully and actually enjoyed the challenge. Just as you exit the hazard, there is a bus stop on the other side and it has been known for waiting passengers to applaud the trainees if they do it well; sadly the bus stop was empty.

Next was a narrow road with speed bumps, lots of them. Here the examiner would be looking for a journey that was as comfortable as possible, this involved gentle braking just before the bump but taking the brakes off as you hit it. If you were still braking as you hit the bump, you risked scraping the front undercarriage of the coach on the road, as the suspension goes down on the front as you brake. I was made aware later, that one driver just went down that road at 30 and the examiner was physically thrown off his seat.

By this time I was totally lost . . . I think this was intentional. The examiner who had been giving clear and simple directions, now asked me to head to a place that was mentioned on an up and coming signpost, "I will not be giving you directions for this part of the test, Jimmy." he said. I noted he used my first name, that helped, 'Darling' would have been better. The idea was to show that I could find my way around, following signed directions and get into the right lanes as required.

We ended up heading towards town and also going under a long tunnel-like underpass, he would expect me to turn my lights on in advance and I had remembered this and did it in good time. I knew I had made mistakes, very minor ones but mistakes nonetheless. A couple of turns later and I recognised the road; it was the one leading back to the depot, was it over so soon? I must have buggered something up really badly to go back early. As we pulled in to the yard, I sneaked a look at the clock, it had been an hour. We parked up and I got out of the driving seat and stood facing him. My shirt was sticking to my back but didn't want to reach behind to pull it away in case the instructors and trainees watching thought this was a signal, besides, my nipples were erect again and I hoped this might influence my results. "Four faults, Jimmy." he said first. I bit my bottom lip; there was no-one else there to do it for me. He explained the faults which included approaching a roundabout too quickly, something I hadn't noticed. It was best not to be defensive about these things and accept the errors as, well . . . errors.

"I'm pleased to inform you that you have passed, well done." he actually smiled at me.

I was just a bit wobbly as I got off the bus and walked slowly towards the gathered crowd with my head low purposely. I had positioned myself in the coach so as to block their view of the examiner giving me my results. As I got nearer, I looked up at their faces grimly and offered my hand to Rod with the words, "Thank you Rod . . . I seem to have passed."

A cheer went up and much back slapping was to be had. I was still recovering from the shock, when I tried to roll a cigarette and couldn't do it, my hands were actually shaking. "Here, have one of mine." offered Rod, I took it, looked him in the eyes and said, "I suppose a shag's out of the question?"

Here ended the lessons. No more training depot, no more two-hour drives to get there and of course, the real work was about to begin, that's a bugger. My wife had better be strapped to the mattress with a deep-pan pizza when I get home.

Now here's a strange thing, I put it back in my trousers and walked in to the depot yard. It was 7am on Monday morning and I was no-longer a trainee, I wasn't a bus driver either.

I reported to the Controllers office, this was a small window in the wall just inside the back entrance marked 'Staff only'. I didn't have a staff, would a tall stick do? Here I learned that I was to spend this week route-learning which involved learning the routes - which seemed obvious really. Next week was the Customer Care course, then more route learning, just how many were there?

Later I was to discover I had made a big mistake. Being new I asked the Controller where he would like me, in the nicest possible way, his gaze passed over my shoulder to a gathering of drivers behind me. "Phil, would you take Jimmy out on route training today?" Phil agreed.

I stood meekly behind him, I was his lamb, he was my Shepherd, I shall not want. This was one of those awkward positions you can find yourself in, tagged up to someone you don't know, eager not to get in the way and not knowing how to strike up any sort of conversation. We went outside. I didn't hold his hand just yet.

"Do you smoke?" he asked "Yes," I replied feeling strangely guilty about it. "Good, have a fag while I check the bus over."

This was odd, my first day and I was asked to have a fag. The truth was he didn't want me in the way whilst he checked the bus - I might ask awkward questions like "What does this do?" or "Should there be blood there?"

He wandered around the outside of the bus, then went inside and pressed all the bells, came back over and got out a cigarette.

"First day then?", "Yes." I replied "Shitting yourself?", "Oh yes" I admitted.

A few minutes later and we exited the yard and headed into the town centre, I had noted that the front of the bus had a destination I hadn't heard of, it can't be local, I've lived here for 30 years.

We pulled up to a bus stop, there was no-one there but we stopped, the doors opened and we waited.

I had been standing up, just a little back from the doors, hanging onto a pole where I could see Phil; my conscience got the better of me. "Should I be doing something?" I asked

"No, not really, you just follow your route notes."
"Right" I answered.

What route notes? I had missed something somewhere but I didn't want to appear stupid, fortunately I had my back pack with me, this usually contained some form of lunch, a note pad, a recently-acquired flask, something for getting stones out of horse hooves (you never know) and a selection of ball point pens in various states of emptiness.

I spent the entire outward journey standing up while trying to write down the directions we were taking. Road numbers, signs, little maps of roundabout exits and pubs. I tended to favour pubs, they were easier to remember. An hour and a half later, we entered the town who's mystery name was on the front of the bus. That was lucky.

It had been an interesting journey from a large seaside town to another large town in the countryside. The route had taken us through tiny villages, shady lanes, wooded glades, Mooreland and secluded forests, the ideal place for burying bodies of recently departed loved ones and business partners.

We had a 10 minute stopover here or as Phil referred to it, "Fag break." I should perhaps clarify for any American readers that 'Fag' refers to a cigarette and not taking some guy behind the toilets and playing 'Hide the sausage'. The return journey was the same, but in the opposite direction obviously. Phil had turned the bus around because it was easier than reversing all the way.

We got back in to our home town and pulled up at the bus stop in the high street, there was another driver waiting for us. I was to learn that drivers stop for lunch but buses don't, the drivers swap over and our bus was to head off doing a different service number, all a bit confusing really. "Meet you back here in an hour then Jimmy." said Phil. "Oh OK, what are you up to then?" I asked. "It's lunch break" he answered. "It's only half ten" I replied "Yep, and we have another one at half past two." "Oh goody, I might like this job."

The day passed quickly thank goodness, we spent the rest of the day doing local routes and I discovered that many of them criss-crossed each other; I could see I would be making some interesting mistakes in the future. My brain had started to crumble by the time we got back in to the yard, it was half seven when we finished, or 19:30 in driver speak and I was truly knackered - sore feet, aching legs and arms weak from hanging on to the various passenger supports.

It was the next day I discovered I had taken the rough end of the pineapple, so to speak. I bumped in to two ex-trainees I knew from previous weeks on the way in to work. I related my story of yesterday's route learning and asked how they managed to face coming in each day.

"You asked the Controller what to do?" he said

"Yes, seemed logical" I answered

"You don't want to do that; you might end up with a driver doing a 12 hour shift"

"Ah" I replied, the other shifts are . . . ?"

"Eight hours" came the reply.

"Bugger, so how do I find an eight hour driver then?" I asked.

"You don't, let control know you're here, just say your name and 'Route learning' and walk away."

"And then?" I queried.

"You go to the high street and spend the day bus-hopping, go where you like."

"And what time can I get away with finishing then?" I asked

"Don't go back to the office before 4.30."

"Bloody hell, you finished at 4.30" I added

"Oh yes, just spend your day sitting on buses, dead easy." he answered

"Sitting"

"Yes, only a fool would stand." and looked at me in an odd way.

I walked inside with them, I had to, I was holding their hands.

"Jimmy, route learning" I said through the hatch.

"OK Jimmy." he answered without even looking up.

I walked away and waited to be called back, it didn't happen, this was too easy. I went in to the room opposite. It was where the proper drivers congregate before going out. Pinned to the walls were notices you were expected to notice, hence the name. These were things like road works, diversions, missing persons, examples of various passes accepted on buses, cheap prostitutes and pictures of buses for drivers with short memories - all that sort of office stuff. I took a copy of every leaflet available, these were to be my saviour, they were bus timetables, what bus went where, when it would get there and a little map on the back showing the route. It was like cheating on an exam.

Next stop, the high street. I jumped on the first bus that came along and said to the driver, "Jimmy, route learning", he grunted. I settled down halfway along the bus. The journey took us to the next town and it was interesting to note that not many people got on to the outbound trip but on the way back it was packed. These were the workers, people who started the day for everyone else, the ones that opened up, turned on the lights and kettle, swept the floors and emptied the bins. I would be one of these people soon. As we came to the end of the route back in to town. I would go and stand by the driver, have a short chat, thank him and get off.

I spent the rest of the week doing this, sticking to the local routes, listening to old ladies chattering about medical problems and the price of cheese. I was starting to develop a technique - learn the route once with notes and then repeat the same route from memory. The third option of walking the route never materialised.

One trip held a little bit of excitement for me, I met a TV star. This gentleman could often be found in late 1960's comedies, he didn't really have major parts but he was a character that often cropped up in things with people like Terry Scott, Peggy Mount and Tony Hancock. His last appearance was in an episode of Doc Martin. He was an old man now, very unstable on his feet, the old ladies on the bus all recognised him and one or two I think knew him reasonably well, they chatted and I was pleased in a way, that he was respectfully treated. One of the old stars that's always worth a nod of acknowledgement without the 'I say, aren't you . . . bit. He died a few months later, he was 83, I'm sure I had nothing to do with it.

The last day of the week and I did a route I had been putting off. This one took four hours to do a round trip, it visited three towns and snaked its way through the back streets and housing estates and worst of all was they all looked the same. Being a bit of a masochist, I did it twice.

The first trip was perhaps the most interesting. Having sat mid-way for three hours, I changed position to the front seats to get a better view, there was an hour's journey time left and we were heading back to base. We stopped in one town for five minutes and both nipped out for a fag.

This driver whose name was Paul, which was his real name too, was far more jovial than the rest, I think it was the clown's costume that did it. He suggested I drove the final leg of the route. Well, give a boy a toy.

Paul knew that there wouldn't be many people to pick up and thought this the best time for 'hands on experience'. Off I set, first impressions were bad, it was like driving a bus trapped in syrup, Paul laughed, "a bit sluggish then". This bus had the acceleration of a brick, it could not get out of trouble, it caused it.

Roundabouts were a problem, this thing needed a days notice to accelerate across them, I spent time rocking forward thinking it would help. Bus stops were interesting too. In training, we pulled in, opened the doors, shut them and pulled off. Now I had to pick up real people, the idea was to pull in, stop (not optional), open the doors and press a button to lower the floor, this was to help the older and less-able to get on, but these old dears were agile, they got on before I even lowered the floor. I almost found myself shouting "Wait!".

Another problem was the ticket machine, this was the first time I had seen the driver's side of it and it was all buttons. Fortunately most of them had free passes, I just pressed 'Pass' and 'Issue' and out popped a ticket but the odd one that paid had to tell me where they were going and I would tap in the appropriate fare stage number. This number could be found by me looking at Paul with puppy eyes and he'd tell me. I also had to handle money too, each driver has a sort of clip-on box attached to the door that held change and I opened Paul's to find it was half-full of Pear drops. "I like pear drops." he smiled "I can, see can they be used for change?", "Don't you dare." he laughed.

Paul also imparted a little bit of ticket wisdom - it may be hard to believe but it has been known for people to use out of date passes, shock horror. The thing is, they know it's out of date and carefully show it with a well-placed finger over the date, tut tut.

I managed to get the bus back to town, it was 20 minutes late but Paul had phoned ahead to warn Control. We both apologised to the passengers as they got off but they were surprisingly kind. "Well he's got to learn sometime hasn't he?" Bless 'em. Paul recommended I do a second trip after lunch and it was a good thing I did.

The second time, it was a different bus and driver. I did the usual "Route learning" gambit opening and sat myself down near the front, perhaps in the hope of having another go behind the wheel. We'd been gone about 30 minutes when the driver made a wrong turn. I said nothing, this could be fun, I thought. The driver went around the block back to where he had come in, stopped and scratched his head in the typical 'Bugger I'm lost' tradition. Unusually no-one on the bus said a word; they knew fun was to be had.

I trotted forward and offered some help, explaining I was new but did the trip this morning. He was grateful, he was a loan-driver from another depot and had only done this route once a couple of weeks ago. I ended up standing the whole route again, but we helped each other and I think I learned more that day than I had the whole week. I just wish it wouldn't keep leaking out.

Chapter seven: Customer care and mentor.

Tomorrow I start the 'Customer Care Course', a 4 day event, and so today I did a little more route learning, it's amazing what you can forget over a weekend. The first trip was out of town and I have already learnt to avoid those lovely, cheerful, lively school children that brighten up our mornings. The little ones are fine, it's the 13 to 15 group that tend to be more . . . verbal.

After the first trip, I find myself back at the stands in the main street of town. It is very odd being let loose on a free rein to come and go as you please. I could have spent the whole time wandering around the shops and no-one would have been any the wiser, I didn't by the way, I get a guilt complex, which can last several minutes.

My third trip out on the day was simple one to a little village just along the coast. Old people in, old people out and the driver was Paul, the guy who let me play with his bus last week. Some drivers just put up with you whilst others make an effort to help out a little, sometimes you have to know where to put yourself. On most runs I sit out the first half, watching the route, land marks etc. and when he/she reaches the halfway point, often a 2 minute break, I will wander up and introduce myself. Here is where you can gauge if it's worth hanging around up front for those words of wisdom. "Would you like to take the wheel?" Paul asked. "Won't you need it to steer the bus?" I questioned. "Nope, you'll be doing that Sunshine" he laughed. Paul was very good and I was pleased to see him again and as we changed places, he introduced me to the whole of the bus. "This is Jimmy, he'll be your driver this morning, he's promised to behave himself!" Laughter erupted.

Well I almost did, I took a wrong turn, and missed another completely but he was happy to share the blame having been distracted chatting to me. Corrections were made with a smile and a quip which helped me to relax a great deal, it is still a strange thing to be driving a bus with real people on expecting it to arrive at their destination roughly on time, and in fact, we did.

Tuesday and back to school: Today is the first day of 'Customer Care' and it's an easy one. We don't have to start until 9am with a predicted finish of 4:30 or 16:30 driver speak, this was something I was going to have to get used to. I even got myself a cheap digital watch that had a 24 hour display window, it would have been fine if only Mickey Mouse's hand didn't get in the way so much.

We assemble in a special room set aside for these courses and we learn that it constitutes part of the way to an NVQ certificate which has now become a requirement under EC law. Life doesn't get any easier.

Today's session covers topics such as fire, vandalism, drunks, ageism, situation control and sandwich spread - topics that are an important part of a bus driver's life. One striking thing is the new ageism laws that are coming into place very soon.

We will no longer be able to address someone in a way that might be insulting to their age, we can't imply a novice is 'Wet behind the ears' or an aged lady might be called 'An old dear' - words that in my eye, are totally harmless. We can say things like 'Daft as a bat' if we can provide proof of the existence of a bat with a low IQ.

I learn to never say sorry: This is so difficult, should you become involved in an accident you must never say sorry, the police and insurance companies would see it as an admission of guilt. This applies also to the person you've just attempted to murder. Don't apologise or give them signed photograph of yourself, they might mention it in a statement, this includes offers to pay for any damage or taking them out to dinner. It is very difficult for any Englishman; it's like not talking about the weather!

Never say sorry again, you're going to die. Now this is a bugger. Imagine shall we, there is a fire on the bus, not the traditional coal burning fire with a grate and comfy chairs sort of thing, but one of those "Oh my god we're going to die." type of fires. Let's assume it's at the back of the bus where they keep the fuel for example, you also have a disabled person on board, in a wheel chair. What would you do first . . . Panic is a good answer and one the coroner would have heard before. The correct answer is getting everyone else, the able-bodied off first.

Sounds a bit harsh doesn't it? The reality is, you're wasting time trying to get the wheelchair out of the bay, assuming the user or carer has thought to let off the brakes. All the while, panic is ensuing and you're blocking up the aisle to the exit. People being people, will start climbing over things, like other people and making the situation worse and we get overcome with smoke and charred a bit. Apparently it smells like roast beef.

Instead, the kindly bus driver will be outside welcoming you into the fresh air. OK, perhaps not, he himself may end up being trapped by the people leaving the bus; his little door opens outward into the aisle you see. What we hope to do, after taking some really good pictures on our mobile phone, is to drag the wheelchair user out of the chair and off the bus. In the worst case scenario; we break the nearest window with the fire extinguisher we just remembered we carried and gently slide (Throw) the disabled person out of the bus. Hopefully someone would have phoned 999, wrapped some potatoes in foil and updated their Face-book page.

Next, spotting a terrorist: After the (what was) recent event of a bus being blown up in London, known as 7/7, we were naturally aware of how vulnerable public transport is and so we had a short course in spotting a Terrorist. It is surprisingly easy, often they will be wearing some form of camouflage battle dress, carry an AK47 and have a Mediterranean appearance. Unfortunately other than the AK47, this description fitted every fifth passenger. This idea was abandoned instead for 'Suspicious packages'.

I have often been suspected of carrying a suspicious package, my lunch box, no, not that one, the other one, with my lunch in. There's nothing wrong with a sausage and cheese sandwich. We, of course, mean unattended bags and we don't mean old ladies sitting alone.

Don't touch bags with wires sticking out or ticking clocks or mobile phones with tape around them, as seen in Bruce Willis films. Terrorists aren't stupid, they're not likely to put cones around backpacks with a notice, 'Caution – Explosive Material' are they? although there is probably some EC regulation in the pipeline somewhere in Brussels. Problem is, bags get left on the bus everyday - how else do you think we get our lunch?

Almonds, explosive smell of almonds - false. I've thrown many an old lady off the bus because her packet of C4 was actually half a pound of marzipan; well it was yellow and smelled of almonds.

Handicapped, is not the same as disabled: We will deal with a lot of handicapped or less-able people, often a person will get on a bus and ask, "Does this bus go to the station?" and the driver will reply, "That's what it says on the front in big letters mate." We have to bear in mind that this person may be visually impaired or simply can't read. Alternatively they might just be as thick as shit.

We had to pass around the table several pairs of glasses, each had a problem, they might have been slightly frosted, deeply scratched, had a prism effect or might just have a tiny clear centre. We were then given the challenge to sort out a handfull of loose change into certain amounts. There were varying levels of difficulty depending on the glasses worn, it gave us a better understanding of other people's situations. I found this lesson of great value . . . I even managed to pocket £1.20.

The sober drunk was a good lesson; man gets on a bus, unsteady on his feet, slurred speech and actions, a typical drunk, or is it someone who's a diabetic low on sugar? Bash him on the head with a bag of Tate & Lyle's finest.

The whole deal was to become a better driver, not a social worker but then again not too far off. That child, withdrawn, never mixes with the others, always last on the bus or uses another stop. Is she being bullied? Or worse (I'll leave that subject unspoken, but you know what I mean.) It doesn't hurt to make a note of it, we're not social workers as I said, but then again, we are human and reporting it to the controllers if you feel something is wrong might make a difference.

The last day was something I really hate, no not finding a pubic hair in the soap, worse than that, Role-playing. This to me, is what Americans do in offices and gatherings of the sociably inept, it's not the British way, we're a shy race, introverted and we like to watch, let's be honest.

We trotted down to the garage and found a double decker bus to act as our stage. Two people were asked to volunteer. Now despite my utter loathing, I stepped forward. I just wanted to get it over with; I sort of knew we would all have to do it. I was selected to be the irate passenger and a female trainee to be the driver. We were each briefed separately as to our roll in this little play. My name would be Evil Bastard.

"What F****** time do you call this, this bus should have been here 20 f****** minutes ago, I'm going to be late for my f****** appointment because of you, I hope you don't expect me to pay for this so-called service."

I might have laid it on a bit strong perhaps. For a moment, I thought the female trainee was going to burst in to tears, her bottom lip started to tremble and she screwed up her eyes, then burst out laughing.

Now credit where credit's due, she tried to pacify me, did all she knew but I was harsh and often spoke over her words, making life difficult, it was fun. The instructor said she had done well, considering . . . he he he.

The instructor took over her part and I re-enacted the role again, here we learned a marked difference. The first was the instructors position, rather than just sitting there, he swivelled around and faced me (and kept a straight face too) he listened to what I said, kept his voice at a low level and was totally calm, because of his lower voice, it put me in a position of having to stop to hear what he had to say, this in-turn made me drop a decibel or two. I still complained but in more constructive sentences and you know, I'm not quite sure how but this feeling that he wanted to be helpful just took over, he's a clever bugger, I'll give him that.

This was the type of thing reflected in the rest of the acting workshop. The man smoking a cigarette upstairs, the mother who refused to collapse the baby buggies to allow another mother to get on, he even offered to hold the baby for her, giving her an option. When people have a choice it opens up a whole new avenue. Another trick, is to involve the rest of the bus passengers, not personally but referring to them, "Now we don't want to hold up everybody do we sir?" sort of thing, this gets the crowd murmur going, a few turned heads and suddenly it has stopped being personal for the antagonist, he's now got a bus full of people to deal with.

The course instructor, who I shall refer to as 'The Course Instructor' was a brilliant tutor, friendly, witty and seemed to take a genuine interest in your views and opinions. His background, from what I could find out, before he joined the bus service was based in London where he had a team of specialist drivers and cars that transported lesser VIPs about town. He and his team were practised in the art of avoidance and defensive driving, the ability of doing 'J' turns, never stopping closer that a cars length to the car in front, making sure you had an exit option, all clever stuff and great fun too but sadly, not something you could do with a bus. It also turns out this was the guy who passed his bus test with zero faults. He's a god.

Customer Care has finished, I am now equipped with life skills, let nothing stand before me, for Jimmy cometh like a tempest on a calm sea . . . if that's OK with you.

Monday, darn, blast and bugger, it looks like the skive is over. Rolled up for work this morning fully expecting to be out on my own route learning, when wham, I've got a mentor. I was as surprised as he was, he hates it. "Hi, I'm Jimmy, your trainee, where would you like me?", "Sat down", was his terse reply.

We travel a well-used route to a major supermarket from the town centre, its pissing down with rain and everyone smells like a wet dog, the windows are steaming up, the heaters on full blast and I keep getting run over by old ladies with their little shopping trolleys. We do this twice more but on the last trip, we stop for two minutes in a back street. The bus is empty and we've got two minutes to kill - fag time. "How's it going?" asked the driver. "Fine" was all I could think of saying, I knew I was in the way. "It's nothing personal, I didn't want to be a mentor, I wanted to be a lumberjack." Poor bugger, must have filled in the wrong form.

After that, we got on fine and chatted now and again. He did let me do the last leg of the journey, town, supermarket and back to town, I know this was a pain for him with me not knowing the fare stages and having to ask him all the time but we warmed to each other. For a guy who hated being a mentor, he was good, passed on some pearls of wisdom as each driver has so-far, and we kept on time. One old lady insisted on telling me she was 92, bless her.

The next day and a different mentor: I wondered if perhaps the last one had requested not to have me again but it turns out he was doing the same route as yesterday and the Control office wanted me to spread my horizons beyond the boundary of the town.

As I boarded the bus, mentor number two who I shall call Gary because I haven't used that name yet, got out of the cab and removed a towel from the driver's seat and neatly folded it up. I gave him a quizzical look, I had one to spare. He went on to explain that as a driver you can be sat in the same seat for up to five hours and the seats are fabric-covered foam and if it's warm you tend to sweat. (Still reading this) Just think sponge, I'll leave it there shall I?

When I signed off for the day, I was given a rota of my duties for the rest of the week. Now at least I will know where I'm meant to be and at what times. Then came the shock, tomorrow starts at 06:27. I didn't know that time existed, it got worse, and each day was 12 hours long.

One thing that annoyed me the next day, sold a chap a ticket, he rode to his destination and alighted (got off!). Now it's common for people to say 'Thank you driver' but this bloke didn't, he said 'Thanks Jimmy'. I know his face from somewhere but dammed if I can remember where, that is so annoying isn't it. Oh hang on, it was my mother's spare son.

I'm slowly getting used to the ticket machine, it's a bit complicated and I'm not going to explain how it works because that's just so boring. There are certain things that keep catching me out, a customer gets on and asks for "The town please" and I dutifully issue a ticket, then he adds "Return."

The free passes issued to the 'oldies', a term we're not allowed to use of course, I prefer 'Low battery life' personally.

These things are a joy to handle, no money changes hands, they get on, tell me their destination and I issue a single free concessionary ticket, I only need to check that the pass is in date and the picture on the pass vaguely resembles the owner, but there is a drawback, they can't be used before 9 am.

Five minutes to nine and I turn into street that 15 minutes ago was deserted and now has a crowd of pensioners waiting at the bus stop. "Oh look, it's the Twirly's" says my mentor. "The Twirly's, what's that?" I ask. "Wait and see" he smiles at me. As I approach, the hands shoot out hailing the bus to stop, I pull in and open the doors. They surge forward as one and ask. "Are we too early?" . . . You may now roll on the floor laughing or just look skyward, it's optional.

One cold morning at some ridiculous time, I had to start my duty in a town 10 miles from the depot. I was to drive to the start point using the shortest route. This my mentor informed me, was 'running light' and so with 'Out of Service' showing on the front of the bus and the internal lights turned off, we had the opportunity to use the A roads, part of which, was a dual-carriage way with a speed limit of 60mph. My mentor, ever aware of health and safety and having a trainee at the wheel of the bus, offered some words of caution for the open road. "Put your foot down Jimmy, we can have a fag before we start."

There is a great feeling you get driving an empty bus on the open road at full tilt; it scares the shit out of car drivers.

We finished the day with another long run well out into the countryside. We started in the town and it was rush hour, it took a full five minutes to load the bus, everyone was eager to go home of course. Most of the people were workers but a few were free pass holders, the retired 'oldies' who are in no real hurry to get anywhere and each seemed to be accompanied by the dreaded two-wheel shopping trolley, this meant that by the time the bus left, it was full and we had another three stops going through the town to stop at.

By the time we loaded up at the second stop, we were up to capacity, this means we had standing passengers who surged forward every time I braked. My mentor decided that we could no longer take any more passengers on-board for safety reasons and so we sailed past the next few stops leaving the waiting passengers behind and they weren't too pleased, especially as this was a half-hourly service. I did feel guilty about this, they could all see my face as I went by, I was a marked man.

If only the 'Oldies' had caught the earlier bus and left this one free for the workers to get home, everything would have been alright. It's not the drivers fault the bus is full or running late but it's the bus driver who gets the blame, of course.

Letters would be written, not just to the bus manager but also to the local paper, each would claim the bus driver ignored them and the bus was half-empty. Fortunately, the management knows this happens and can check the on-board cameras to confirm the situation. Imagine looking at the video and seeing someone's face pressed against the camera.

Another day, another dollop: My mentor had been taken ill, I wondered if it was those mushrooms I gave him - the bloke in the market said they were magic mushrooms and I knew my mentor was good at card tricks and would perhaps appreciate them.

One of the controllers had to drive the bus, which was fine with me; it was late and getting later.

The bus was crowded with old people who had thoughtfully had put their shopping trolleys in the wheelchair and baby buggy section. We had a problem; a young mother with a buggy was waiting at a bus stop. The buggy would have to be collapsed and put in the luggage rack along with its bags of shopping. Deciding to be of some use, I offered my assistance, took one look at the buggy and offered to hold the baby instead, its less complicated, father of three speaking here.

Another hold up came in the countryside. A young lad had started feeling sick and we were miles from anywhere, we stopped at one of those old battered wooden huts that pass as bus stops or 'Love cottages' and he went behind it to throw up. We were nice about it and didn't drive off but it did end up adding another five minutes to the 20 minutes we were already late.

We got back to town half an hour late and worst of all, half an hour into what should have been my lunch break. I trotted in to the control office and explained about the late running and was given my hour back and instructed to spend the afternoon route learning on the one service I hadn't done.

This service was the long distance one that straddled, one of my favourite words, two counties two cites and over 20 towns and villages. It took six hours to complete and was driven by only a select few, I guess those with the best bladder control led the field here. At the appointed time, I got on-board, told the driver I was route learning and dashed quickly up the stairs, the last thing I wanted to do was stand on the platform chatting all the way.

I settled down at the front to enjoy the view and what a view it was, this bus travelled along part of a route I knew but from my vantage point I could now see over the high walls and fences into peoples gardens. There were other interesting moments too that I never knew about until now, by riding on the top deck. Trees, yes, those woody things sticking out of the ground, I was convinced the bus would hit the lower branches, it didn't but it should have, same with traffic lights on corners, the bus turns at the last moment, narrowly avoiding the things. This to me, was like some funfair ride, and the bloody thing swayed in the wind.

We stopped at a bus station about three quarters of the way along the route; I took this opportunity to jump off and stretch my legs and have a crafty fag. Bus stations usually mean a stop over for five minutes and it turned out to be a good thing I did, the driver was packing up his stuff.

"You've not finished have you?" I asked suddenly feeling I was about to get stranded. "Oh no, just a 30 minute rest break, EC rules", "Ah, I see" I lied and followed him up to the rest room, eager not to let him out of my sight, as he was literally my ticket home. Here, he explained the driver's hours for long distance driving which I didn't really understand and I explained about losing my mentor for the day. "Looks like Control just wanted you out of the way for the rest of the day then" he said. "Seems so, but at least I'm sort of doing something useful, learning the route." I replied.", "Not really, it'll be dark in an hour."

Well that was a waste of time, not that I was too bothered. Back at base a few hours later signing off, I heard a voice call my name.

"Your name Jimmy? Jimmy" said the voice behind the glass. Ever wary I replied "Might be.", "Your uniforms here", "In that case, it is". I was quite excited. I phoned the wife and told her tonight was dressing-up night; hope she still has that nurse's uniform.

Friday and I turn up for work in my nice new uniform, I felt like it was my first day at a new school - I was starting to fit in or perhaps 'blend in' would be more appropriate. I was immediately called in to the Controllers office; I'd been there so often now, I had my own mug.

"Can I see your licence please Jimmy?" said the plump controller. I can't call him the fat controller; I think that one's already taken.
"I lent it to an Arab friend" I replied. He just looked at me with his head to one side and a raised eyebrow; I caved in and gave it to him, and the licence. Turns out we are periodically checked to make sure we have a current one. I knew mine was fine; I'd only printed it last week. "Don't go yet, I have something for you" he added. "Oh Chocolates, you shouldn't have bothered." I answered. "I haven't, you didn't put out" he replied, he was catching on. "Here you go, try not to sell it." He handed my very own module. This is like getting a medal except it isn't. The module was a sealed plastic block about the size of a packet of fags, its purpose was to record your actions on the ticket machine and tell you how much to pay in at the end of the day. I felt there should have been some sort of ritual involved, rolling up a trouser leg and bearing a breast and maybe being tapped on both shoulders with an Austin Mark IV starting-handle but it wasn't to be.

I was also given a pad of emergency tickets with strict instructions not to use them unless . . . yes, you've guessed haven't you? Next was a cash box, pear drops not included. I finally left the office equipped and clothed by the company, other than my underwear and back-pack, the company owned 90% of me.

I had a new mentor too, his name is Dave, it's his real name too, he'll be so pleased to read his name in print, he'll buy several copies I'm sure. Dave was easy-going and relaxed, he let me drive all day.

I made a wrong turn and had to find a roundabout to turn around in but the passengers were very good about it, Dave unlike the other mentors, buggered off down the bus and started chatting to the passengers and made a joke about my mistake. To be honest, this was possibly the best thing he could do, not the joke bit, the leaving-me-to-it bit. He wasn't looking over my shoulder, which took a lot of pressure off me. I could see he was a popular driver with the passengers, most people complain that the drivers are grumpy gits and I could understand that, knowing what they have to go though.

As I was leaving for the day, one of the controllers called me aside, aside isn't my name but I answer to anything these days, ticket machine training had been arranged for Wednesday, he also gave me next weeks rota and it turns out I don't go back to work until Wednesday, looks like a five day weekend for me, I was also asked which route I knew well enough to drive on my own and I had to admit to just two. I knew more but they still had tricky bits, like the wife. I have the feeling I'm going to be chucked in at the deep end.

There are a few things people don't know about bus stops and yes, I'm going to tell you - boring. The bus companies don't own the bus stops, it's the council, it's the same council that puts the flag post at one end when the bus stops at the other end, it's the council that puts the shelter at the wrong end so you still get wet going to the bus entrance, it's the council that put little wooden huts along the road with no side window so you can't see the bus coming, its the council that puts them directly after pedestrian crossings. You're starting to get the picture now I guess, but I've saved the best 'till last. You'll never guess what bus stops are for . . . yes, buses, the clue are the big yellow letters saying BUS STOP, not 'Cash Point nearby' or 'Just popping in to the chemist' or even 'Picking up my pizza'.

Another thing, I'm on a roll here, Request Stops, other than Bus Stations, all Bus stops are Request Stops. The idea is, you see a bus coming along, its a happy bus, you can hear people singing inside, the driver is smiling and it goes sailing by you,

'Oh bother!' you may say to yourself, 'that handsome bus driver with the flowing golden locks has accidentally driven past me, never mind there'll be another in 20 minutes'. The reality is, the driver doesn't know you want the bus, you didn't put your hand out. Many a time I have pulled in, opened the doors and the potential passenger just looks at me, or there's a couple chatting and just happen to be standing at a bus stop. Mind you, in the town I come from, people talking to posts and telegraph poles is normal. So just remember, to stop a bus, put your hand out or throw money in the road . . . unless you're an old lady, then just walk out in front of it waving your stick. OK, rant over.

After five days off, its back on the road with my favourite mentor, Dave. (He's probably bought another copy by now) and we're off into the countryside on my favourite three hour jaunt. Its mid-morning and people going places are already there and so we have an easy time ahead of us, or it would have been if it hadn't started raining. This route involves hills - you know, those lumpy things in the countryside where they put trees, it also has valleys, like the gap between bosoms, they tend to go hand in hand.

One section, has the road carving a snake-like curve through a wood with tall earth banks and trees blocking out the sky, creating a tunnel-like journey, it's twilight time, very Gothic and slightly sinister. I don't know why but I feel at home here. Is this relevant at all? Well yes, be patient.

Trip completed and arriving back at base, we set off to find some lunch. Dave has his own and I check out where the most seagulls are congregating for some free bread.

Our next journey is back to where we've just been After about five miles, we hit the countryside. It's throwing it down, the sides of the roads have become little rivers and the windscreen wipers are doing an Irish jig. Having climbed the biggest bosom - sorry, hill - we slowly descend into the valley. What a difference a couple of hours of heavy rain can make, the tree tunnel had become a carpet of wet leaves and broken branches. The earth banks had turned the water into a muddy river and were threatening to collapse into the road, the village at the bottom was flooded and the council was out poking sticks down the drains.

We meet one of our buses that was on its way back, it shouldn't have been there, it was half an hour late. As it approached, I could see the driver slide his window back, Dave told me to slow down and draw level with it, the driver wanted to tell us something. It turns out that there was a huge flooding in a dip further along the route, so deep that he had to wait for the council to unblock a drain before attempting to go through it. What I didn't know, was that the air that powers the brakes is sucked in underneath the bus into these large cylinders and if you go through deep water, it will get sucked up inside, causing the brakes to come on and they won't go off until an engineer can clear it. We were advised to go with caution, which meant seeing if the car in front got through without the water coming above the wheel hub. The good news is we made it, pity.

Oh dear, I seem to have broken a bus. It wasn't my fault, honest. I was proceeding in an orderly fashion, when just as we were turning across a major junction, a buzzer sounded and sounded. Constant would probably describe it better. A red light appeared on the dashboard and I summonsed my mentor who was chatting to the passengers with the gentle cry of . . . ". . . Help, we're all going to die.", actually, I used special code words "I think we have a problem."

"Do the brakes work Jimmy?" asked Dave, the collective hushed silence was deafening. "Yes." I replied after a suitable knicker-gripping pause. "Pull in at that bus stop just there." He said calmly.

Dave noticed that air tank number one was a tadge low, a tadge being a technical term; it's a bit like a smidgin, but not a shinny. We called Control and an engineer was arranged to pay a visit. We had a handful of old ladies on the bus who took this in their stride, knitting appeared from nowhere and Mrs Smith went on to tell Mrs. Jones in great detail, how her daughter-in-law's child birth went, she wasn't there but she knew all about it, after all, she was a mother of six.

Had this been rush hour, the younger people would be ranting and raving, telling us how important it was to get to work and we'd be trying to calm them down with how important it was not to die.

15 minutes later, the engineer arrived and started delving under the engine cover at the back. Meanwhile, I flagged down the next bus and transferred the passengers on-board.

It turned out that an old repair to an air hose had failed, this was kissed better by the engineer and we drove back to the depot. It is perhaps gratifying to know that air brake failure will make the bus stop and not, as many may imagine, run out of control.

Chapter eight: Who's a big boy then?

I was off to the city, me and Dave, or is that Dave and I? Grammar had never been my good point. We waited at the bus stop to take over a bus, we had bus driver uniforms on and so we thought this the best option. It arrived on time, several people fainted, I myself felt a bit giddy. It was a double decker and I'd only driven one once in the training depot yard I looked in the cab, then back at my mentor, "Go on then, get in" said Dave, full of confidence, he must have been holding mine because I couldn't find it. I slid my module into the ticket machine, no foreplay here, keyed in the running numbers, adjusted the steering wheel and seat position, looked at Dave and said "Tell my wife I love her." and prepared for the off.

Now, if I'm perfectly honest, I was nervous to the point of squishy trousers. This thing was massive with an upstairs, but maybe you knew that. I expected it to be sluggish and heavy to respond but I was mistaken. This thing shot off the moment I touched the accelerator. The brakes were pretty good too when I applied them, it was like the world just suddenly stopped revolving, freeze-frame. I saw Dave in the rear view mirror turn to the passengers and say, "Sorry, new driver" this seemed to give me carte blanche to make a few mistakes.

I was ever-conscious of the extra height above and I knew the route itself had no hazards like low bridges or cables but for some reason I kept looking for them. For the next half hour or so, I took things very carefully, it was silly really, the bus was the same width and length as a single decker, in fact it was slightly shorter by almost a smidgin. What I think was playing on my mind, was balance. What if there were too many people on the top deck and not enough on the lower, making it unstable? I had this stupid idea that it would topple over on a corner. It didn't fall over of course, that sort of stuff makes the headlines and I can't remember one story of it happening - hitting bridges, now that's another thing.

The city was a challenge. It was full of buses vying for position and I ended up the last in a row of five, with no option of passing. As we neared the city centre, it became a bus only-road which you'd think would make it easier, it didn't. The council had redesigned the area and dropped the kerbs to level with the road; this removed a psychological barrier to pedestrians which meant they just stepped out in the road in front of you. Cyclists wove their merry way with complete disregard for anything and the odd skateboarding student would pass by on the outside. The city centre averaged one accident a week and three fatalities a year.

On the way out. after the Valium had kicked in. I met my first irate passenger. Trundling along the main road out of the city. a man runs out into the road from behind a parked bus and waves us down. "You were going to f****** drive by weren't you?" We tried to explain that we can't see through parked buses and that it was up to him to make himself more visible. He apologised and thanked us for explaining it to him. Did he buggery! I remained calm and asked him where he wanted to go; the change of subject was enough to dampen his ardour, which I think is a small breed of dog. One thing on the way did make me smile. "A return please driver" said the man of advancing years
"Certainly sir, where to" said the kindly-faced driver. "Back here of course." came the reply. Can't fault that now, can I?

My first accident: I had been driving faultlessly all day and was finishing my duty with a local route which took me over a level crossing. These crossing gates had a reputation, once down they stayed down until at least three trains had passed by, enough time to allow a long line of traffic to build up on all sides. Eventually, the gates went up and we slowly filtered over the lines, praying the traffic lights on the other side stayed green, like you do. I turned into a popular town road that was chock-a-block with traffic waiting for their light to turn green.

The gap between me, the parked cars on my left and queuing cars on my right was minimal, bordering on impossible. I edged my way forward and the queuing cars nudged their way slightly outwards creating just enough room to ease through, great attention was paid to my mirrors, it was imperative I kept the bus straight, a slight deviation would bring the back end out and much scraping would ensue.

There was a dull thud. Dave was standing a little behind me, waving out the window - it helped him pass the time and he came up front as I stopped the bus. A small sports car was diagonally across the front of the bus, it wasn't there a few seconds ago and curiously, there was no-one in it.

Looking to our left, we could see an empty parking space. Could someone in the line of traffic opposite have decided to dive in, failed and abandoned the car where it stood? Impossible of course, it could not have happened in the short moment I had looked away in my mirrors.

I phoned Sherlock Holmes but he was busy sniffing bicycle seats in the name of research. We'd have to sort this out ourselves. When we got out of the bus, we discovered a black mark on the lower nearside bumper of the bus, one that could only have been made by a tyre, a car tyre.

How would that get there? Unless . . . the penny dropped, I pushed the car, it moved - the handbrake was off. This car wasn't where we found it. It had started off as a parked car on our left amongst the other parked cars, not noticeable except that it was parked badly. By badly, I mean at a slight angle in the parking bay with its front wheel poking out. The driver hadn't bothered to straighten the steering, let alone the car. As the bus came along, and my attention was elsewhere, the front of the bus hit the sticking out front wheel and as the hand brake wasn't applied, the car literally rolled out in to the road in front of us. We pushed it back and it fitted perfectly.

We moved off as we were holding up the traffic and pulled in when we found a gap. I left a note under the windscreen wiper of the car asking the driver to contact the depot, as there had been a collision with a bus.

Nothing ever happened about it. I wasn't surprised, I had noted the number plate which was a custom one with altered lettering, what should have been a five had been turned in to an 'S'. The tax had been out-of-date too, this person wouldn't be claiming anything, it shouldn't have been on the road, not that there was any damage, we only hit the tyre at walking speed.

So, what's in store for me in the near future, well, I can tell you . . . they're sending me out by myself on Friday. Yes, you read that right, my mentor Dave is quite happy about it, one of the controllers is happy with my progress and is aware that I'm not one hundred percent confident but perhaps feels I need a bit of a push, which is fair enough. After all, I've been having just too much fun so far, and so we fast-forward to Friday.

Today I was unleashed on to a very unsuspecting world at the crack of dawn, well, 6:35 am anyway. I had been talked into 'Giving it a go'. As one controller told me, "Would you consider going out by yourself on Friday?" was the suggestion put to me at the beginning of the week. "Don't worry if you don't feel up to it yet." came her next line, after I filled the gap with a long pause.

Feeling that this was a challenge, a gauntlet if you like, trust in my face but wrapped in pink ribbon. What man would admit that he felt inadequate about something to a gaggle of controllers? I accepted.

Friday and I arrived at 5:45, a little bit too early but I had the chance to grab a coffee and get my running board and fault card. The running board is simply a list of instructions and route timing stages. I sat down in the car with my steaming coffee to 'Study the form' - what time I should be on my way, where I was going, what to do when I got there, what to do when I got back and when the first break was. Now I found it easier just to look at what is on the ahead side of the break period, the rest can be studied in the break itself, no good overwhelming myself with too much information is there? break it down in to manageable chunks, something my wife whispered to me one night.

The fault card told me the fleet number of the bus and the controller thoughtfully told me where it was, in this case, the back of the garage. I toddled off towards the bus with 20 minutes in hand; there was a reason for this which I shall reveal now . . . everything about setting up the bus for its first trip had, of course, leaked out of my head.

My first problem was finding the thing, all buses look alike. I knew it was at the back but so were a dozen others; a dozen is 12 for those metric people amongst you. Having found it pretending to be a tree, I pressed the Emergency door button and they swished open, so far so good.

First stumbling block, where the hell was the cab light

switch, I'd never used it yet, this was embarrassing, there was no way I was going to ask Control. I'd look a right ding-bat. Much fumbling was to be had before my world lit up.

I stuck in my module, no that isn't my wife's pet name for my willy. Having set up the ticket machine I started the bus. Now was the time for the first check, a walk up the bus pressing the bells was easy, as was opening the emergency door and listening for the alarm to sound in the cab. Next, a visit outside.

Standing in front of the bus confirmed the lights were working, next the windscreen, yes; it had one - that would save my hair being ruffled up. A walk around the thing confirmed that it generally had a wheel near each corner and nothing was hanging off. I had to note down all dents and scratches on the fault card, this would take the blame off me from any previous driver's mishaps. Next I had to water it.

Yes buses need water, not just for the engine but for the heating too. It was here that mistakes could and were made. The water cap is directly above the fuel filler cap, they are very different in design but some drivers had been known to use the wrong hole. Notice no wrong hole joke, it was so tempting.

It was time to rock and roll. I was alone in charge of a bus, just me. My solitude was short-lived, there was a customer at the stand in town, for goodness sake man, it's half-past bloody six, who starts work at that ungodly time . . . er . . . yes, OK. The drive was totally uneventful, sort of. This journey was one I thought I knew well, but there were moments when I thought 'Where the hell am I?' until I spotted a familiar landmark. Dave had been wise in his words, make note of landmarks along the route but make sure also that they're ones that will still be there a week later - an empty packet of crisps by the road side was a no no, whilst a building like a church was a yes yes.

This route included an historic town and it was with some relief when it came into view, this was two-thirds of the way. The town itself, was on a hill with a huge Manor house, several churches, loads of antique shops and 15th century thatched cottages, they were like little houses with 1960's Beatles-style hair cuts. It was these I needed to avoid, they tended to overhang the narrow roads and knocking them down was frowned upon.

I made it to the far-end and had a calming fag. The trip back was uneventful until I reached the outskirts of my home town; it was 9am, time for the free passes to begin. By the time I pulled into town, the bus was full; I opened the doors and let out the fragrance of lavender and mothballs. I knew the last leg of the journey had been a success, all the old dears had been chatting away oblivious of my driving, had the bus been silent then I would know I was doing it wrong, old ladies are a good measuring stick.

After lunch, or should that be brunch? I was set to do a local service, four times. I was quite happy about this; I used to live in that area and knew the roads well except for one drawback, the level-crossings run by Mr. Bastard.

This duty meant I had to cross them eight times. I joined the back of the queue with 11 cars in front of me, I already knew if the gates went up and the lights turned green only five cars would get across before the traffic lights went red again. After only a couple of minutes, the gates went up, the cars moved forward, five cars crossed with another two going through the red light, as they do. I was within reach, the next green light would see me across . . . and Mr. Bastard put the gates down again.

17 minutes we waited there, the record stood at 21 minutes. Four trains passed, I noted a four minute gap between them. Mr. Bastard was on a roll. This crossing used to have its own signal box but that was removed years ago and I have yet to find out which other box Mr. Bastard hides in, I'll bet it's that one with the bullet holes in.

Boy was I late and there was no chance of making up time, the route meandered all around the back streets and the only long straight road had speed bumps in, 11 of them.
By the end of the four runs, I came in just 10 minutes late. Not sure how that happened. Feeling a little guilty, I apologised to the next driver with the words 'Level crossing, sorry', he smiled, he knew. Things couldn't get any worse.

Ha bloody ha. My last job of the day was a simple trip to the next town via a shopping estate on a major road and through a village. It was rush hour and my fan club, sorry, passengers were all heading out of town going home, I knew that, they were smiling.

The shopping centre was no problem; all I had to do was cross the main road and head into the village. This village isn't a cluster of buildings but a line of houses along the one single road. The road had no footpaths and the buildings formed the edge of the road, it was a tight squeeze at the best of times. This however, wasn't the best of times. There had been an accident on the main road and those with local knowledge, diverted down into the village.

The lane was packed, the high flint walls all seemed to lean out into the road, traffic-calmers made it even harder to pass, chuck in a few vans and you have mayhem. As I slowly passed, one van the driver shouted at me, "In your own time mate." in a sarcastic voice and they wonder why the van THEY are driving is covered in dents and scratches, bits of bumpers missing from their own bad driving and anyway, it's a work van so it doesn't matter does it? Try saying that to a bus driver in charge of 12 tons of metal valued at £100,000 or more. Once the pressure was off, I got back to enjoying the driving, I started the day in the dark and I would end it that way too. My trial by fire was over.

Chapter nine: I'm a bus driver apparently.

Monday morning, my rota says turn up for work at 06:49 and so, being one who hates to be late, I was there at 06:20 having a coffee and listening to the gossip. As it drew closer to 06:49 I started to worry - my mentor Dave hadn't turned up yet. I approached the controller's window. "Dave's not turned up yet?", "No, he's got a day off today, ballet lessons." he replied. "Oh, who's my mentor for the day?" I enquire. "You haven't got one; you're on your own."

Something damp trickled down my leg; I hope it was wee wee. I knew I was starting the 'Nursery routes' next week but I had assumed until then I would be under someone's wing, turns out they were obviously impressed with my work alone on Friday and brought it forward. Bollocks, they were short-staffed.

I found the bus, big oblong thing and sorted it out, got to the stand five minutes late, no-one was there, phew, I could easily catch up at that time in the morning. Fortunately, I had my street notes and stage stops list for that route in my bag, which was very lucky for me, otherwise I would have to make it up and there's no fooling passengers, I would look a bit stupid getting off at every bus stop and looking at the time table and map wouldn't I?

I only had two routes that day, which repeated several times each. All in all, I got on with it with no real problems, the controllers asked if everything was OK at lunchtime and I had to admit that they were. Tomorrow, a day off, I can cry then.

Mid week trauma: He is aged about 7 years old, just a kid with a stick playing in an alleyway until I pass and the little bastard throws a stone at the window, and more by luck than judgement I should imagine, he broke MY bus.

As I approached a well-known supermarket just out of town, a fellow driver coming in the opposite direction, pointed to this child at the end of an alleyway on the road, I nodded that I understood to keep any eye on him as I will be coming back that way in a few minutes. I assumed it as a 'watch out for the child in case he runs out in the road' type of warning.

As I passed, there was a dull thud and I slowed down, I had seen the child as I approached and he ducked back in the alley, safe to pass I thought. Two old gentlemen, oops, not allowed to be ageist now are we? Two males who were entitled to free travel on the buses due having reached the state retirement age, called out that a window had been broken and that they thought it was the young child I had just passed.

I was now on the approach to a roundabout and had to move past it and pull over. I got out of the cab thing and looked at the damage from inside and then outside, stupid really, what difference would there be?

I asked the two males of 'Pass holding acceptance' if they actually saw the child throw the stone, they were not sure. I know how one's mind links one item to another, but I needed an eye witness and unfortunately these two were not 100%. I noted that they were sitting on the other side of the bus, a small child outside would not easily be seen from there. I'm sure he did it, just as much as they are but one element of doubt and that's it.

I apologised for the delay and asked them if they had any injuries, one informed me he had shell shock in 1944 but other than that, he was OK. I told them that I would take them back to the bus stand we had just left so they could get another bus, it had a shelter and was starting to rain, and I also wanted a reason to go back that way.

Off I set, very gently, when a big chunk of the glass fell out. I stopped and told them that I could go no further in this condition. Luckily, a bus pulled up behind having seen me stopped in the wrong place with the hazard lights on. I explained and he took my passengers on for me.

I called control to let them know what had happened and they asked me if I could bring it back to the depot. I said I would have to knock the remaining glass into the bus but it was not a problem, they asked me to be careful - who said controllers had no hearts? Oh yes, that was me.

I got back and they handed me another bus, not as nice as the modern ones I'd been driving but it allowed me to carry on, which I did, it was my job after all. It was only later that I thought I could claim trauma damage and plead for psychiatric counselling, everybody's doing it these days.

Another day, another challenge: As you have may have picked up, I live in an area that has a lot of historical interest and today saw me heading to one place that was crammed with it. As I approached the town via it's very narrow roads, I stopped at a pedestrian crossing just before the town square where there was a small crowd of people, OK, four, waving me down to stop. My goodness I thought, or words to that effect, I wonder what these people want and why they are stopping me here where there's no bus stop. I soon found out after I picked them up. As I rounded the corner I almost killed a whole table full of marmalade, it was market day and no bugger told me.

Heck, I thought, how do I get out of this one then? My eyes eventually saw the hand-written sign, 'All traffic', pointing to a very narrow gap between two buildings, would I fit? Yes, about six or so inches each side, not a problem. Where the problem started, was leaving the narrow gap. I needed to get at least three-quarters of the bus out of the narrow lane before starting a turn or I would end up wedged, somehow I managed it and I have to admit, I enjoyed the challenge even with the risk of huge embarrassment if I got stuck. I do see the funny side of things I have to admit, that's why I don't work for a funeral directors - Imagine me turning up for work with a 'T' shirt emblazoned with the legend 'I See Dead People'.

Heart stopping moment of the day, a football rolls across the road under the bus, fortunately the children didn't follow it. No, I didn't flatten it, I tried.

Bus companies have been investing in new low-floor buses, I think there is some new legislation coming in, forcing this change. there is also some directive to local councils, asking them to raise the kerbs at bus stops - this is like inventing a spoon with a hole in the middle. I do wish they'd talk to each other sometimes.

Halloween: It's nearly 11am in the morning, I don't start until three in the afternoon and have to work until midnight and it's Halloween. I wonder who or what is going to step on my bus tonight. I'll take some garlic with me and a stake, well a hamburger at the very least.

Later that same day, I had been warned by other drivers that it was some sort of tradition for kids to throw eggs at passing buses, why eggs no one knew, it just happened. I suppose it was better than body parts. Everything went well until the evening.

Sure enough passing a pub, a first for me, along came these two eggs, one on each side of the windscreen, I instinctively ducked, a natural reaction, I was lucky not to crash the thing, I was also lucky they were just eggs - in this town it was likely that they'd leave the eggs in the box, or worse, the chicken.

The kids had scattered and what could I do anyway. I turned on the wipers and discovered why eggs were used. I sat and watched as the windscreen became smeared, making it totally opaque like a frosted bathroom window. Worse was to come, the screen washers were empty; obviously someone hadn't topped them up on first check. I would have to improvise. There was no way I could pee that high but my bottle of blackcurrant juice did the job in the end, trouble is moths kept getting stuck to the windscreen now.

Later that evening, I'd started to pick up the party people heading towards town. A couple of mummy's, the bandaged sort, a skeleton, a Dracula and his victim and a fairy. Where the fairy fitted in I'm not sure but she did have good legs, they went all the way to the ground. I resisted asking old ladies that got on if they were going to a zombie party.

The rest of the evening was uneventful and I got home at half past midnight, jumped into bed and woke the living-dead.

Brass monkeys. All of a sudden, it's winter, a frost on the car windscreen and a really cold breeze welcomed me. My morning was spent on a local run and it was a most uncomfortable morning to say the least. The reason, the heater didn't work. I was lucky in the route to pass a local playing field that had a toilet, that cold weather has an effect on me - ever tried holding a cocktail sausage with oven gloves? at least ladies can hover above the seat. To make things worse, I'd put my thermal Long Johns on the wrong way round in the dark - no wonder I couldn't find the willy hole. Back at the bus, I rechecked for any levers that needed to be pushed to get the heat flowing, no joy. I suffered that morning, the really strange bit was, after the sun had been up a while, my head was getting hot but my feet were freezing. A fault card was filed with a shaking hand that morning.

Personal hate: Modern cars with clear indicator lenses rather than the traditional yellow ones, these cars have a yellow light bulb instead, and if you're at a slight angle, as in approaching a roundabout, you just can't see them as clearly as the older ones. The other thing are car drivers who just have no idea how a roundabout works, I sit there waiting for them to go as they approach from the right, and the buggers just sit there, looking at ME!

The wee hours - there seems to be a common theme here. At 06:19 one morning, I found myself just out in the countryside running light to a distant village with a dire need to 'powder my nose'. One thing that we have not been taught, is how to control bodily functions on a cold November morning. Public toilets, not a hope, all locked up and rarely is there one near a bus stop, one has to 'improvise' and not get arrested at the same time. As I was a little early, I parked up in a lay-by that had a good range of bushes and shrubbery. The bad news - I would have to find a place that was not lit up by the bus lights or passing traffic. My luck was in and relief was at hand, how the hell do other drivers manage? I soon discovered when I got back to the depot and asked them.

"Plastic drinks bottle Jimmy" said an unnamed driver. "The thought had crossed my mind but. . . ", "With a wide neck obviously" he added with a knowing smile. "The deckers have cameras all over the place" I retaliated back at him. "Not if you stand halfway up the stairs" he countered back. "And the single deckers?", "You're buggered" he laughed.

He also advised using a bottle that used to hold yellow or orange - coloured juice, as it might look suspicious leaving a bus with a blackcurrant bottle with yellow wee wee in it. Thank god I didn't ask him about number two's, an image of a cake tin came into view.

This will be controversial, I expect. An interesting point was raised one day recently whilst I was hiding amongst a group of drivers. A woman enters a bus wearing a hijāb, one of those where you can only see the eyes and offers a bus pass.

The pass has a full face picture of the holder printed on it and part of our job is to make sure the holder bears some slight resemblance to the person depicted. Asking them to lift it up is out of the question and refusing travel would be seen as racist, religious-ist, or some form of ist.

There are augments against not allowing travel but she may not be the person depicted, she could even be a he for all we know. It's not personal or political, it's just bloody awkward.

Heard my first bus joke today. What do you call a bloke with a bus on his head? Dead. It's not tasteful but it is funny.

One of our bus stops is missing. There's this village, yes another one, we're surrounded with 'em, but this one is a bit on the posh side, no vans in the driveways unless they're getting their pool cleaned or a new rosette cabinet for their daughter's pony's trophies You can tell the status of a place by its bus stops. My home town for instance, has concrete posts with anti-vandal paint, villages generally have what can best be described as wooden sheds similar to those found on allotments and cities have perspex art-forms, totally impractical but they look nice.
This village had beautiful wooden shelters, summer-house-like even. Stout, wooden uprights that must have been six inches across, crafted planks with turned edges, a bench as thick as a thick thing, even the roof was made up of curved edge overlapping wooden squares, it was a joy to behold.

You may be wondering why a bus even goes through a village like this, a bus service would be beneath them or so you would think, the truth is, these are rich, retired people and rich people are incredibly tight which is why they're rich. I myself, have seen a Jag come out of a driveway ahead of me, only to find it a few minutes later parked up the road and the occupants waiting at the bus stop with their passes in their hands. Anyway I have digressed.

One bus stop was missing, it was there yesterday, it had been there a while in fact, but today it was gone, and freshly gone at that. The clue was in the bushes that surrounded it, they still held the shape of the missing shelter and they hadn't eased forward to start filling the void. I pondered the problem for a while and came up with a plausible solution.

Stealing this shelter at night would have raised much suspicion with passing dog walkers and nearby residents; it wasn't something that could be done discreetly. So, steal it in the daytime.

Turn up in a truck with one of those folding arm hoists, attach a couple of straps and lift it out and onto the truck - time required, about 10 minutes with two blokes. Don't be silly, you may be thinking, stealing something right in front of people's eyes just won't work, yes it will if it looks like you're meant to be doing it. Two blokes, hard hats and yellow vests, professional tools, it must be a council job, no questions asked and if they were, then it's being taken away to be refurbished - simple.

Something I forgot to mention the other day, I had the opportunity to see just what is recorded by the cameras on the buses. The guy who was showing us, wanted the drivers to see exactly what was recorded in the event of an accident or incident, it was reassuring.

The bus in question, had seven cameras in operation, the outside ones see the front, front side and back view, so if a car hit the front, another camera would have caught its approach. Internal cameras also have a view past the passengers and out the windows. The cab camera catches a view through the entrance doors, almost every angle is covered, this is ideal if it shows a car driver cutting a corner, speeding, on the wrong side of the road etc.

The screen also shows the time, when the brakes were pressed and what indicators were on (or off). I was amazed at the quality of the imagery as well, full colour - and to top it all, these cameras operate even when the power on the bus is turned off as in overnight. A very useful insight indeed. So don't try nicking one, you'll end up on You Tube.

Many people have made claims against bus companies, the most common, being a fall on the bus followed in second place, by whiplash. The fall claims go unfulfilled if it shows the customer moving around whilst the bus is going or getting up before the bus stops, you wouldn't get off a ride at an amusement park before it stops would you?

I know of a whiplash claim that was made by one young mother with a buggy who, when out of sight of the driver, was recorded by the bus behind showing her running across the road with the buggy, she dropped her claim when we passed-on the video to her insurance people.

I've been exposed! A chap at work has informed me that the little blog I keep as a bus driver has reached the higher echelons of the management system, the ones with the more expensive suits, they quite like it, 'amusing' I think was the word used.

There is an undercurrent of concern about what I write. We have all heard stories in the past of bloggers being dismissed or taken to court because they have been stupid enough to write down things that are, well, inappropriate, inaccurate, slanderous, or salacious - there, you thought I couldn't spell half of those, didn't you?

When I started this blog, I looked at the two ways it could be presented. A behind the scenes anonymous type of thing giving the gritty day to day, blow by blow account, or the simple straightforward ramblings of a mild-mannered, middle of the road guy, looking for the simple things in life. I chose the latter; I didn't want my testicles nailed to the back of a bus.

I'm glad this issue has been brought up, in a way. I can reassure those concerned, that scandal, scaremongering and undermining is not my cup of tea, there's enough crap around, why add to it? So I shall continue in the vain that I have started, lightly amusing, mostly factual and unbiased.

You will have, no-doubt noticed, I haven't mentioned the bus company by name or names of drivers directly, to be honest, they're all the same, it can apply to anyone, and any company whatever industry. Apart from that, they're reading this!

I shan't mention which Controller has a passion for knitting, who is a transsexual, the one with very neat eyebrows and walks like he's chewing a toffee with his buttocks is a clue, nor will I allude to the guy who's built a scale model of Tower Bridge from navel fluff and ear wax, donations gratefully received, ask for Norman. This paragraph might be fictitious by the way (or not).

Why me: I got lumbered with an oldie, not a person, a bus, 'Pride of the Fleet' are words not mentioned in its presence. What drove me mad, were the windscreen wipers. It had started raining and so I put the wipers on, as you do. Now modern buses have wipers that swish almost noiselessly across the glass in harmony, some however, had a tendency to judder, making an annoying noise which you sort of get used to. This bus had neither, this bus had independent wipers, each had its own motor I was later to discover. Everything started off fine, then I noticed they started to get out of sync, what started out as going left to right as a pair drifted in the a Mexican wave style and then into a clapping action. Luckily they didn't cross over each others paths otherwise they would have knitted a scarf.

Chapter ten: Mobility scooters & bus stops.

Mobility Scooters: I hate the bloody things. In principle, they're a good idea and a godsend to those with real mobility problems and a solution to those that are too lazy or too fat - there, I've said it.

Let us assume that the elderly lady owner of a new mobility scooter has never driven anything faster that an egg whisk. Her dead husband did all the driving, but the smell was getting too much and so she had to bury him. We're talking about people of an age where this was the norm, I think they used to call them housewives.

Now suddenly, Mrs recently-widowed was in charge of a machine capable of speeds up to eight mph in public. Little (if any) training, arthritic hands on the controls, milky eyes, reduced hearing and a penchant for the occasional blue rinse at the hairdressers - his is an accident waiting to happen. A physically fit, fast reacting teenager has to undergo a series of tests and lessons before they're allowed on the road with a moped. OK, once the teenager is on the road, they go wild but mobility scooters are wild from the start.

I have enough trouble dodging them on the pavement when I'm walking, let alone having one zoom off the pavement in front of the bus and trundle along in front without a care in the world. Hand signals, forget it, mirrors rarely fitted, lights yes but not used (they drain the battery you know) reflectors, not seen them, large flashing beacon on a pole would be ideal, restricting them to pavement use is the answer. I'm not a killjoy, just amazed nothing serious has happened yet. I have been informed that some have even tried to get on a bus with them!

RTA (Road Traffic Accident) Sorry, not politically correct anymore. We all have become acquainted with the acronym RTA through TV programmes like Casualty and the like, but now they have to be called RTC (Road Traffic Collision) as it has been defined that accidents don't happen, there is a reason or cause behind them, let's just forget that you may not be the cause, that the other driver pulled out in front of you, or the tree fell down, or the earth opened up in front of you, surely an accident is an unexpected event? I know one of my daughters was, only joking, I wouldn't swap them for anything. (Still pondering that last sentence).

Free Passes on the buses: Bus drivers love the free passes, no money to handle, the elderly, infirm and many others have this benefit of free travel around the county, wonderful, allows them to keep in touch with their diminishing number of friends, or just get out for a while and wave at them in the cemetery as they pass. What can be a little awkward, are those that try to use them before 9am. We try very politely to explain that they just can't be used, it's a council rule not a bus company one. "But I need to be at the doctors' surgery by half past eight dear, my colostomy bag is full." Some do get most irate about it but the machine just can't issue a concessionary ticket before 9am. I am often tempted to ask what they did before free passes.

I did sit down one day and work out how much money they were saving in a year given three trips a week at a basic £3.10 return to town, it works out at around £465 per year and they begrudge £1.20 to the local doctors' surgery. Gift horse and mouth come to mind. Oh yes, we're used to the five minutes to nine trick of trying to keep the driver talking too.

Why's the bus not moving? The bus route is divided up into sections and the start of each section is a timing point, the bus is meant to arrive at specific times at these timing points. If it arrives early, it has to wait until its allotted time then move on, known in the trade as 'Fag time'. In rush hour, the bus can often not make these times and sails past if the stop is empty or the person waiting there is ugly and a danger to small children.

Nothing for ages and then three at once. This is a classic and yes, it happens, we've all seen it and I will try to explain. We're going to be here a while, get comfy.

Scene one: Three buses going along the road, one answer is each bus has a different destination but at some point they just happen to use part of the same route, a big clue will be the number displayed on the front with the destination. We're sorry, all buses look the same don't they, do feel free to stop the bus and ask the driver, I can see his smiling face now.

Scene two: The first bus hits 9am and the Twirlies (Too earlies) start getting on at each stop slowing the progress of the bus, then chuck in a couple of traffic lights and it's 10 minutes late. The next bus behind, now starts to catch up and the nice driver will try to overtake the first bus and ease the other driver's burden and so they end up playing leapfrog along the route. There are even cases where the bus in front has pulled in and the second bus is just about to go past it, when someone will pop out from behind the first bus and put their hand out, stopping the second bus which has to pull in. Bus number three is on its way, the driver is wondering why there's no people to pick up, eventually as the bus in front gets later and later, he catches them up and tags on to the end, he can't overtake because he's on time and so this bus is annoyingly empty.

There are occasions where the driver of the third bus will phone up the control office and ask permission to go 'Out of Service' and will drive past the other two buses and go back into service a couple of miles further ahead. This helps to take the strain off the other two buses but is very annoying for any passengers along the route seeing an empty bus go by them without stopping.

This, of course, doesn't always work. If the third bus has just one passenger on, then it has to stay behind and stick to the timetable.

No bus driver wants to be late, it's just as irritating to them as it can be to the passengers, but in his case, being late means he will lose a chunk of his lunch break as will the next driver he hands over to, unless he can make up time.

Scene three: Roadwork's, temporary traffic lights, stop/go boards, badly parked lorries, railway crossings, accidents, wheelchairs, less-able passengers, diversions, cars parked in bus stops, buses parked in bus stops (it happens), road resurfacing, groups of foreign students buying weekly tickets, parades, processions and protests, old slow buses, fires, lost passes, lost people, lost children, urgent toilet break, someone taken ill on the bus, dashboard warning lights requiring the bus to stop and reset - these are some of the things that can slow down a bus. OK, serious bit over, let's lighten the mood.

I don't know what it is, but bus stops appear to have an odd magnetic attraction for just about any vehicle except buses, and one day one of our drivers waiting at a bus stop to go to work decided to play a game when a car drove in and stopped in front of him, he got in.

"Single to the town centre please." he asked the car driver. "What?" replied the driver, somewhat taken aback. "Single to the town centre, if you'd be so kind.", "This isn't a bus." said the now agitated driver. "You're in a bus stop, you must be a bus.", "I'm going to the cash point" he replied. "You'd better take out an extra £70 to pay the fine for obstructing the bus stop when I report you." said the bus driver and got out. "F*** off" said the now red-faced car driver. "Yes you'd better" answered the bus driver. The people at the bus stop clapped, they loved it.

It's 9:20 am and I'm having a nice cuppa at home while getting ready for work. Packed lunch, lucky teddy, four-leafed clover, spare underwear, stun gun. I was all set when I heard a tornado warning come over the radio on the local stations breakfast show. Now what the heck are military aircraft doing flying over the coast on a day like today, it's raining hard and very windy outside. Not the ideal weather for aircraft, I would have thought. They don't mean a Tornado as in . . . weather do they? surely not . . . they bloody do. I hope I'm not driving a double decker today, not in high winds; I'd better look for the rubber underwear with the elasticated leg-holes.

Driving a high-sided vehicle in strong winds is a nightmare, it's like walking in the wind, holding a large sheet of hardboard in front of you - you're buffeted from side to side. Everything is manageable until you hit a gap between buildings and it rushes at you like a crowd of rugby players looking for the bar, it's funny how your bottom starts acting like it's sucking a lemon.

The drunk: I manage to throw a drunk off the bus this week. It can be quite intimidating the first time. Said drunk rushed in 'I've got a pass' he said and went and sat down. I carried on sorting the rest of the crowd out. All done, I leaned out of the cab and said 'I'll have to see that pass sir' . . . nothing. Keeping my cheery persona in full-flow, I flounced out of the cab (you can't get out of a bus cab gracefully, I can assure you). "May I see your pass sir?" He sat there motionless, eyes looking up at me. I paused, the bus went quiet and this puts the pressure on him, now he's become the centre of attention. Keeping my voice at normal level, I asked again. He opened up his hand and flashed (wait for it) some form of ID in a small plastic wallet similar to that of a bus pass. "Sorry sir, didn't quite catch that", I moved a little closer. As he opened it again, I shoved my finger quickly in the open pass book. "That's a British Rail pass I think you'll find sir" (British Rail went off the tracks years ago). "I'm afraid I'm going to have to ask you to leave the bus sir . . . pause . . . unless you can pay?", I stepped aside and amazingly he got up and left the bus.

A bit of a non-event really. What surprised me, was the ease with which it worked. Sure, once off the bus, he became abusive but I just closed the doors and left. I've done a few night buses now, taken a few that have had too many, but in most cases they seem to slip into automatic and pay or show a pass, they don't set out with the intention of not paying, it just slips their mind at times and needs a small prompt. Yes, I do remember in training that we should ignore the drunks but I know there's much entertainment value to be had and the passengers love it, so do I.

We have been requested by members of the public and local residents, that when a bus is 'standing', that is to say - we have to wait for a certain amount of time before moving off, that we should shut the engine down. A request which we are more than happy to comply with, but it has one drawback that I discovered one morning.

I could not understand why people kept asking me the number of the bus. We're not allowed to say, "It's in big yellow letters on the front." because some of our passengers may be partially sighted, and so we tell them the number and in which direction it is going.

It was later that day, when I was forced to have a fag break because I was early, that I discovered that powering down the bus also blanked out the display at the front. What I do now is shout out the bus number every 60 seconds and people passing by think I'm a deranged bingo caller.

How to piss off a disabled person: I'm sorry to say that there are certain people who abuse the system and make things difficult for others. I had to turn off a main road into a narrow side road; this road had a cycle lane on the left and double yellows on the right. I could see a car parked over the cycle lane, just in the area I need to complete my turn; I could also see that someone was sitting in the driver's seat.

I brought the bus up behind the parked car and tooted my horn, nothing, I tooted again. The arse end of my bus was still sticking out in the main road and traffic was building up. The car driver glanced into their wing mirror and did nothing. I tooted again, this time a double toot, again I was ignored, but was drawing attention from shoppers nearby.

Shortly and pre-empting my third toot which would have been followed by a personal visit, an aged man strides across the road, opened the passenger door, reached in and removed his disabled sign and waved it at me. Now I am not casting aspersions on what his disability may be, we could all clearly see he could walk with no apparent problems. I was prompted to say out loud, more for the benefit of my passengers and the watching public, "You're still required to park without hindering or causing an obstruction to other road users . . . Sir." There was a good chance that the disabled person was actually the car driver and not the passenger.

Now I'm not getting at the badge holders because they're badge holders, I get very annoyed when I see a four by four pull into a disabled bay, the driver, clad in a track suit, jump out and dash up to the cash point machine. I think these people should be glued into a wheelchair for a week and see how they like it.

It's not just the disabled, I notice more and more the mature driver, a person of standing in the community, park their car on the bloody pavement. Now how will a young mother with a child in a push chair get past? By going into the road. All this makes my blood boil, I could go on but I'm going for a lie down instead and stick pins in this wax doll I've been making.

Going spare: I didn't touch a bus today, not that bus touching is illegal you understand, just frowned upon. It would appear that a past error on my rota has had a knock-on effect and so today as I reported for duty, there was nothing allocated to me.

I was to become a 'spare', left to loiter around the depot, waiting for another driver to be stricken by consumption or a life-threatening splinter in a pinkie.

The day was not a complete waste as the controllers, in their collective wisdom, decided that I should go forth and learn the extra-long route I started to learn to a distant major city. I think they got fed up with me talking to the vending-machine. This was the route only selected drivers drove and I got halfway before darkness fell. I donned my trusty bus drivers garb and sallied forth.

As we ventured into new ground, I looked at the 'Drivers notes' and tried to follow the route, drawing a rough map as we went. I noted down important signs along the way, No Parking, Keep Left, and Give way etc. The end depot is small but perfectly-formed, not unlike my wife, who was looking over my shoulder as I wrote that bit. The driver's rest room had carpet on the floor instead of sawdust, the toilets were designer stainless steel, all lovely and clean and there was even a special room just for reading or relaxing without the distraction of vending machines or the TV. Yes, they have moving pictures over here now.

Break finished, we set off on the return journey. It was like a different journey, the landmarks I had noticed on the way in were different, we were of course approaching from the direction now, and it's like learning two routes at once. I was starting to wonder if I was being groomed for this route.

New Year's Day. Went in to work this morning and guess what, I wasn't listed to work that day and they sent me home. I told the controllers I loved them and left quickly before they changed their minds.

This week I'm working the AD rota. AD stands for As-Directed and not Anally-Defective as I suspected. This means I do whatever the controllers want me to do, such as keep out of their hair - if they had any. I fully expected to be here there and everywhere. It's not uncommon after a festive break of a couple of days that a driver or two might be a little under the weather and staff shortages ensue, but no, the cunning buggers had other plans for me.

I was, as I had suspected, to learn the long-distance route again but this time I was to be driving it. I was to be given a pilot, he was known as 'Dan Dan, the Pilot man'. He seemed unfazed with my lack of route knowledge and so off I went whistling 'Fools rush in'.

The whole trip took nine and a half hours including two one-hour breaks. It made a nice change from the usual around town routes and you really felt you were driving somewhere - I was starting to like it. Two more piloted journeys and I was let off the lead to fend for myself, I had become 'One of the few'.

I'm starting to get the hang of this service now, it still has its moments. Last night I was coming back along an open stretch of road at 50mph when I got caught by a gust of wind, I almost has a trouser accident I can tell you, I wonder how I would have explained that to Control.

"Control here, Mick speaking"

"Hi Mick, Jimmy here, I've er. . . had a little accident"

"What's the damage?"

"It's a . . . . spillage"

"Can you mop it up at all?"

"Not from where I'm sitting"

"Ha ha, you make it sound like you've shi . . . . "(Pause, small light bulb appears)

"Oh"

"Hmm, yes . . . . Please, don't tell anyone"

It could have been a lot worse of course.

"Hi Control, Jimmy here"

"Hi Jimmy, what's the problem?"

"The bus fell over"

Shorter, I think you'll agree, but I think the trouser accident could still be part of the scenario. Still, it didn't fall over and my pride remained intact, I just slowed down. If you have a feeling of déjà vu it's because this was at the front of the book to make you moist.

Chapter eleven: Beer, Sweaty Betty & lost.

I seem to be retarded! Unbeknown (long word of the week) to most passengers buses and trucks are fitted with a brake retarder. This is usually an electro-magnetic device fitted around the drive shaft that comes into play when the brake is depressed, as in pushed down, not as in sad. This device slows down the drive shaft to assist in braking, exceptionally useful when driving downhill. The effect of this on the bus, is the sensation of a suddenly hitting a giant elastic band stretched across the road, similar perhaps to the wire across the decks of aircraft carriers to stop the landing planes from shooting off the other end and becoming submarines. So if you experience a jerking sensation on the bus, it's this that is the cause, unless you're playing with yourself.

'As a judge m'lud': I always get that sinking feeling when I walk past the controller's window and I hear "Ah Jimmy - just the man." I sense the other controllers sniggering in the background.

I manage to pull myself away from an interesting conversation about a dalek and a dustbin and stick my head through the open window. "You have been selected for an Alcohol Breath Test", I was informed. "Oh, right - that should be fun", replied I. For a fleeting moment, I thought that I might be plied with a volume of selected ales to make sure the machine works, that thought didn't stay long, pity. I was to be tested by Mr. L who is the only controller with his own pen (the others are on lengths of string) and a witness, Mr. H who had recently sharpened his pencil and was handy and not walking around with a clipboard.

Many people assume that drivers are ordinary men and women, which of course they are, but they have to go through a lot to earn that badge and random alcohol and drug testing is part of the package.

I was escorted to a private room where I was exposed . . . to the machine, exciting isn't it? It resembled a cross between an asthma breath tester and an old police breathalyser. Mr. L showed me a sealed disposable mouth piece that would be inserted into the machine - it was the wrong shape for anywhere else. Next the machine was calibrated so it displayed 'Insert 10p to start'.

"Blow slowly and steadily until the buzzing sound stops", I was instructed "And you're not to hold the machine in any way." It was a really a strange feeling standing there, hands behind my back and I couldn't stop thinking that all this could be a practical joke and I was being filmed.

The buzzing stopped, the pause seemed to last a lifetime . . . "Negative." said Mr. L, did I hear a note of disappointment from him? Now I knew I had nothing to worry about and all this was an adventure to me and so I could look at the whole thing in a light-hearted way but there is, of course, a serious side to all this.

I asked what happens if it had been a positive result. It turns out that there would be another test in 20 minutes time and whilst waiting I would have to be escorted around if I required a drink of water or needed the toilet, basically under 'house arrest' in a way. A second positive would result in instant suspension and disciplinary action. Can't wait for the drugs test!

Early one morning, just as the sun was rising, sing-a-long now: Its 5:10 in the morning on a cold, damp December Monday. I'm due to start the route at 5:20 but roll the bus out in to the street to give some space in the yard. It gets a bit cramped first-thing with drivers running around shouting 'I can't find the bloody thing'.

One thing I do enjoy about doing the long service run, is the diversity of habitat I drive through. Town, village, city and countryside. I have been fortunate in having the ability to enjoy nature in it's rawest form, the wildlife observations have been fantastic. Sure, they have been flattened out of shape in most cases but tyre-marks aside, nature's creatures have a beauty about them.

One of the stops along the route is the cemetery, often a little old lady will get on and ask for a return ticket to the cemetery, I resist the temptation to ask her if that's a wise investment.

One of the many things that perplexes me about the elderly and infirm, is after struggling to get on the bus, they insist on wobbling down to the far end. I watch them carefully in the internal mirror taking care not to move off until they have sat down. I will admit to one moment of weakness where one old dear just hovered above the seat for what felt like an eternity. I pressed down on the foot brake, released the hand-brake, re applied the hand brake and released the foot brake. This had the effect of giving the bus a slight judder, enough to plop the lady in place and we could now proceed onwards.

One chap, having mislaid his free pass, had to pay cash for his journey but he was 20 pence short of the fare, I suggested he run alongside until the next stop, we laughed. I meant it.

An incident occurred that is worth a mention. It happened at a bus station where the buses have to draw in face-first, this means that when loaded we have to reverse backward (is there any other way of reversing?) from between other buses until well past them, then hand brake on, out of gear, hazard lights off, audio reversing speaker disengaged, re-select forward, brake off and advance. All this whilst triple-checking the mirrors and stuck out in the middle of the forecourt like a little island.

This irate customer came storming across, arms spinning like a demented windmill in the air before him, he of course wanted to get on the bus, I waved back at him indicating that I would NOT let him on and he came around to the side of the bus. I again indicated that I would NOT let him on, and even said out loud "I'm sorry sir, too late." This was for the benefit of the passengers more than anything else.

He pressed the 'Emergency Door Open Button' on the outside. "I'm sorry sir, I have started a manoeuvre I can not stop from this point." He ranted and raved about waiting 40 minutes for a bus and was very verbal. Knowing that the only way I could stop him was to allow him on, he had already climbed on the bus at this point, I told him to "take a seat; I'll deal with you when I stop next."

Now you may think me a little harsh and perhaps a bit of a 'jobs-worth' but once we have closed the doors it's a rule not to open them. We have a poster in the depot telling the story of an accident along these lines involving the death of a child. It was some time before I had to stop again to let someone off and he came up to me, still red in the face. I asked him where he wished to travel to and dealt with the ticket. Whilst sorting it out, I told him that I could possibly lose my job over an incident like that, he went back and sat down. When he eventually got to his stop, he apologised to me, the air was lifted as he explained it was his anger at his bus not turning up. I gave him the telephone number of the bus station and recommended he contact them and perhaps there might be a valid reason for the delay. I have picked up this passenger twice since this event; he always makes a point of saying a warm hello to me and I of greeting him.

'Out of service': Someone had 'Parked a tiger' or as it more commonly known, thrown-up on my bus. If it had been a child, they would have, of course received much sympathy, "Ah, poor thing" being the usual comment but this was an adult and so everyone quickly concludes it's the Black Death all over again and attempt to set fire to the culprit. I manage to get everyone off the bus with a promise of free money so I could go back to the depot and have the bus cleaned.

I have a lot of respect for the cleaners at work. They have to deal with a lot of shit, often literally. "So, what's the best way to deal with sick then?" I asked, genuinely interested. "We take the seat outside into the yard and put some bread on it." he answered. "Right and that soaks up the sick does it?" I said amazed. "Nope, the seagulls come down and eat it."

Today as I waited, a chap got on and said "Hello Jimmy" this, of course throws me - another one of those 'Who the hell are you?' moments had arisen. It turns out he was someone important within the company. "Hi" I reply, "Do I know you?" I bravely ask. "I'm someone important within the company, I read your blog," he answered. "Oh, I'm so sorry" I said sheepishly and added, "But there's no picture of me", "No, I worked out what your rota was and where you'd be today."

"I haven't got much money." I replied. "It's OK, I'm just a stalker."

I was to develop a friendship with 'Someone Important within the Company Person'; he was intelligent, witty and prepared to come down to my level. He said my blog gave interesting insights into the company. When I got home I re-read the thing and removed anything incriminating against me.

A rose by any other name: I picked up 'Sweaty Betty' as she is known. Few words can describe Betty, unwashed seems inadequate, witch-like seems unfair to witches and holocaust victim is politically incorrect. Betty is a tough call, she's entitled to free travel and will always offer you her pass but none of us want to touch it, even the inspector will pass her by. We can and do refuse travel to certain people. Betty has been banned several times in the past, due to her odour and attire which leads to fellow passengers getting off the bus before their stop, not good for a bus company but this time she was on a stretch of open road between two towns which was unusual for her and so I stopped to pick her up. I do have a soft side, don't tell the wife, she'll start expecting flowers.

Fortunately, she went to the back of the bus but I could hear the windows opening and the hiss of handbag sized perfume sprays scenting the air, now I was driving a perfumed boudoir! Betty, or Sweaty to use her first name, got off a couple of stops down the road and we carried on as normal.

Arrived at the final destination, a well known seaside resort and parked up for the few minutes I had spare to do a jigsaw. As the last passenger left, they remarked that there was a smell emanating from the back of the bus. Now I had the unenviable job of feeling for a wet seat. It was dry and a quick spray with a mini deodorant spay I carry for such occasions cured the problem. For some strange reason on the trip back, I was followed by a herd of wild musk oxen.

Wednesday wasn't a good day for me, apart from it having more letters than you actually pronounce and being the marker for the middle of the week, it had done me no favours and today was no exception.

I was on the long distance run and had reached the halfway point, when I was informed that due to a bomb scare, I was to divert around the motorway that I would have normally been joining. "Just turn right at the end of the road, over the bridge, first left at the roundabout, follow the road to the level crossing, bear left at the fork in the road and straight on until you reach the petrol station, then left and left again to the roundabout, that'll take you back on route." he said, I didn't take in at all. All the while he had been explaining, he'd been holding an imaginary steering wheel and doing the turns as he went along.

It was easy for him to say he'd been saying it all morning, but to me, this was uncharted waters but a saviour was at hand in the form of a lovely woman passenger of unbound cheerfulness and ample bosom.

She offered to take me in hand figuratively speaking – (it was our first date mind you) and guides me thought the traumas that are the back streets of this county. After a while, I started to recall certain roads and realised that I'd been here before as a trainee driver and should I have to come back that way, I'd have a good chance of getting it right. I did ask the woman, no I begged actually, if she would like to stay on the bus with me but she had to go off and have her cleavage buffed up.

On my return journey, I stopped off before committing myself (don't answer that) to joining the motorway. I asked a fellow driver. "Ain't got a clue mate." came his reply - you can see an Oxford education wasn't wasted on him. I phoned Control, no answer. So looking at the motorway from where I stood and seeing moving traffic, I thought, well it must be clear now and went for it.

No sooner had I joined the slip road that I saw the signs, single lane ahead and a build up of traffic, bugger it. After a short distance, a slip road appeared going to my left, it seemed familiar; memories of the training bus came to mind. I slipped off the motorway, so did everyone else.

It took two and a half hours to get back to the bus station at the halfway point, a distance of less than ten miles. The poor controller who had sent me out, was surrounded by bus drivers all smiling and asking where they should park the bus they've just brought in late. Due to this route having European driving regulations applying, we had all overshot our rest breaks and had to have 45 minutes 'standing down'. I popped into town looking for an Ann Summers shop in the vague hope of bumping into an ex trainee bus driver to humiliate.

On my return, I handed him my running board and bowed before him. He quickly deduced that I had 30 minutes left to cover a three hour journey. He pointed to a line of buses that had been parked up in the railway station across the road. "Take number xxxxxx" and go straight home. "I'll never get that parked outside my house!" I answered. "Just f*** off, please." Now that, I understood.

My day was looking up. There is an old bus driver's adage, 'An empty bus is a happy bus' it was so true. We found out later, that the suspect package that had caused so much mayhem, was in fact nothing more than a bag of builders waste with some electrical wires sticking out of it.

Arriving back at base just 10 minutes late from my due-time having had the luxury of running 'Out of Service' on the A-roads. I handed over the bus to the next driver. He hugged me in a brotherly way but I did sense he was a little excited. The other buses were coming in over an hour late.

End of day: cashing up time or what really happens to all the money. All I had to do was pay-in. As you sign off the bus with a few keystrokes a ticket is printed telling me how much I need to pay in.

Most drivers have a float, no not something that hangs around after three flushes. Personal cash, an amount of their own money that goes in the cash tray at the start of the day to enable them to give change. When you pay-in you should take out the float and the money left over should match what is printed on the end of day ticket. Does it buggery, its often short, very rarely is it over. If it's short, you have to pay in the balance from your own pocket unless you can stick your hand in another drivers pocket without him noticing.

How often have we heard, "Oh, I'm 20 pence short driver", still - the company has lots of money, they won't miss 20 pence will they?" No they won't, we have to pay it. We're not unsympathetic, it's just we can't afford it.

An oldie but not a goldie: "You've got the slow one today Jimmy," informed the Controller, "but at least you won't be caught running early with it." I thought I had driven the oldest bus in the fleet, I was wrong. Now at first sight, this double decker looked the same as all the rest, in fact, they all looked the same to me, but as soon as I stepped inside I knew - because . . . there were steps! The others have the low floor easy access layout, not this bugger; you had to climb aboard in every sense of the word.

I flipped a switch and turned a knob in the usual starting process, nothing happened. There should have been a shudder followed by a chug chug as the engine caught hold and kicked into life but nothing happened . . . hmm, perhaps I had to fill it up with coal first, I thought. Without the engine running, I could get no internal lights to function to see the dashboard. Then, lit up by the glow of my growing embarrassment, I saw a button marked. . START.

Bingo! - Houston, we have ignition. The whole bus lit up like a 10 watt bulb in a distant fog a long way away, I actually thought it got darker when I flipped the cab light on, a faint yellow glow bathed the reins, I mean steering wheel. I noted that somehow, the few remaining empty buses had edged away - spooky.

Well, I suppose I'd better find out what-does-what. As I looked at the dashboard, I saw the speedometer was marked in Roman numerals, no surprise there then. I did spot a rev counter with 'Isambard Kingdom Brunel – made in the British Empire' stamped on the faceplate. My next task would be to walk around the inside of the bus to check everything was intact. I saw a long piece of string running the length of the bus with a loop on one end; I assumed that the loop was placed over ones genitals and a swift tug given by the passengers as I approached their stop – only kidding. Did I mention the windows were made of lead and stained glass? Inside inspection done, I jumped out to check the lights and bodywork.

The headlights were fine, one kept going out but I trimmed the wick and it was fine. The indicators – one red flag and one green one were there and the general bodywork and ramparts seemed in good shape. On my way back to the cab, I tripped over a brick tied to a length of rope, the hand-brake I presumed.

The engine had been running for about 3 minutes, I checked

underneath to see if anything had fallen off, nope, it all seemed to be holding together. I'd better get moving then and take it outside and park it on the road for a couple of minutes in readiness for the off.

I might have exaggerated a bit here and there but you get the gist, it was an OLD bus, however, looks can be deceiving - just ask my wife. It may have been a bit sluggish to start but once it got to twenty . . . it stayed there.

In reality, it was a good solid bus, slow yes, but not unpleasant to drive and it made a nice change - well worth the £30 quid scrap money.

Taxi: You either love them or hate them, a bit like Brussels sprouts I suppose. I have a growing dislike, I'm sorry to say. They had never bothered me before, until I started to drive a bus. One taxi and one bus stop, the driver, in urgent need of a newsagent, must have been running low on Jelly babies, just stops at any place convenient to him, even if it is a bus stop and on the wrong side of the road too. Just next to the stop, is parking for the shops and around the back, a bigger, free car park. Funny how you never see a bus at a taxi rank but I sorely tempted.

Talking of taxi ranks, which I wasn't but I am now. On the way out of the town centre we have to pass out of the end of the pedestrian precinct, which narrows down, and passes between two lines of cars. On our left are bays for blue badge-holders whose cars are often at the most peculiar angle, (still amazes me that they drive these massive 4 X 4 jeeps) and on the other side taxis lots of 'em. Now generally it's not a problem, just take it carefully but for one small thing. When two or more taxi drivers are gathered, gossip prevails and to this end, each parked taxi has its window down and a fellow driver will be stood next to it chatting, and they're standing in the road, and when a bus comes along, do they move? . . . not bloody likely I get closer to their bottoms than their favourite brand of toilet paper at times.

I have this vision, that one day I shall drive past so close that their trousers will be ripped away to reveal half of them wearing stockings and suspenders and yes, they're all blokes.

My, how I shall laugh. Benny Hill, eat your heart out, oh bugger, forgot he's dead.

Risk: Took a big risk last week that no bus driver should ever take . . . I had to do it you understand, I had no choice. I know I may be ostracised' (exercised whilst dressed as an ostrich, I think it means, I may be wrong), but temptation got the better of me . . . I opened and ate a sweet given to me by a UFO that had been sitting in my cash box for over a week. UFO - Unusually Friendly Oldie. Normally we welcome these small offerings with thanks, assuming we know they are fresh, it's the small sweets that have us worried. Just how long have they been in that pocket? we wonder. Anyway, I needed something and took a chance. It was lovely but I've never seen one like it before, it was a Fox's Glacier Mint but it was black and tasted of aniseed. I hope that was normal.

Off on a tangent again: I've not been to a concert for years, I've seen people as diverse as The Shadows, to Frank Zappa, with a sprinkling of Status Quo here and there but it looks like a new 'rock' group is about to burst on to the stage - I've started to see the signs everywhere . . . so keep an eye out for 'Loose Chippings' coming to a town near you.

Naughty naughty: The boys in yellow strike, yes, it used to be the boys in blue but now every bugger wears these Hi Vis vests, so much so that they no longer stand out as they have become the norm. Anyway I digress, the point being that just the other day, there seemed to be a bit of a blitz, Police and Traffic Wardens all over the place. I watched one car get booked for parking in a disabled bay, another in a loading-only zone and what I enjoyed most, a woman getting a good talking-to for parking at a bus stop and leaving the car unattended with two children inside.

Chapter twelve: Mr. Twat & groupies.

I had a crap day by the way; you are permitted to say 'Awww'. It started out well enough, set off on time and everything but got held up a lot, darn highwaymen. Most of the problems were road works which were in full-swing, unmanned but in full-swing and when I arrived at mid point, I was 30 minutes late, leaving me just 20 minutes to find food to eat or a McDonald's, whichever came first. I got comfortable and watched the traffic drag by a new junction layout being built around the corner from the bus station. Is it something to do with daffodils? I wonder. As soon as they appear, workmen and JCB Hybrids invade the streets and rip them to bits.

As I mulled this over, I took out my running board to confirm what time I took over the next bus to come home and shock horror, I should have arrived at 11:26, and there I was eating lunch at 11:05. I checked my watch, I checked my mobile, 11:05 it was, oh bugger, how have I managed that?

The Rocky Horror 'Time Warp' song filled my head - there's ample room and it won't disturb any dust. Deeply concerned (ha ha) I wandered back to the bus station and bumped in to a fellow driver. '"Have the ticket machine clocks on the buses ever been wrong?" I enquired in my best quiet voice. "Yes, it has happened." he replied looking at me strangely, he had no choice, he was ugly. "Oh, I seem to be here half an hour early." I said. We were talking within hearing distance of the duty controller, he flicked his eyes up at me, I caught them and handed them back.

"Are you sure you have the right running board?" asked my fellow driver, I pulled it out, the running board that is and showed him. "That's the wrong one." he said, "!" said I.

It would appear that I still had yesterdays board in my bag, the one that's half an hour later than today's which was tucked behind it, I did feel a fool but he didn't mind. Its amazing when you try to reason something out in your head you miss the most obvious.

On a lighter note, I awarded a prize to a passenger as she got on with the words "You win today's prize for the best wave at a bus stop!" we laughed, her bosoms bounced.

Got Lost: I was to do a route I hadn't done for ages, a four hour circular and I had trouble remembering bits of it but managed to bluff my way so far until I hit a housing estate. Every house was identical, the gardens were open-plan and mainly laid to grass, no plastic pink flamingos or garish gnomes to lead the way, the landscape was devoid of note.

My concentration was broken by a chorus of "We don't go this way, driver." Oh dear. I was just about to pull up at the far bus stop for some quick thinking or possibly burst into tears when I heard one passenger say to another "He'll have to turn at the roundabout at the top." This was greeted with several hmm's of acknowledgement from others.

I have to say; when it comes to the crunch, at least the passengers know where to go. Duly armed with this wisdom, I set off, my mind trying to calculate if I could get the bus around the mini roundabout at the top in one go, when as we drew up to a set of traffic lights, a passenger suggested I turned off and used a road that had been used as a diversion some weeks before. This clinched it for me, I knew that I could get a bus down there, problem solved and a look of surprise as I pulled up at the right bus stop where only a few moments earlier the waiting passengers had seen me turn off away from them, they looked at me knowingly and smiled . . . well, we all make mistakes, its getting out of them that counts and we all had a laugh - at my expense, of course.

It's been a funny week, a bit of this, a bit of that, very little of the other. I am still seeing an amazing number of car drivers still using mobile phones. Some have taken to cupping their hand around the phone so that they think it can't be seen. If only they would realise that moving their mouth is enough to give the game away, gesturing with the other hand is a good clue too.

A driver related a wonderful story to me the other day which I shall tell you about, it will lack the original zest that was told in but you'll get the gist. . . .

Once upon a time, a car driver decided to pull into a bus stop to complete an important task such as rent a DVD, go to a bank machine or order a pizza, he had assumed that these tasks placed him above the traffic law. Along came a bus a little bit early, the driver was now required to wait for a couple of minutes at the bus stop that was occupied by the car. We're not allowed to leave a bus stop early as you know, unless it's on fire.

The driver, being a sensible chap, parked as close as he could alongside the car to cause the least obstruction to the traffic flow. Along came the car driver, "Can you move your bus?" asks the car driver, "Not for two minutes." replies the bus driver. At this point, the car driver decides that he must insist that the driver moves the bus, the driver again politely replies in the negative.

The car driver who we shall now refer to as Mr. Twat now boards the bus and instructs the driver to "Move." but perhaps not so politely, again the driver declines. The driver is safe in the knowledge he is doing everything right, being polite, informing Mr. Twat that he has caused an obstruction by illegally parking at an operational bus stop but most of all, keeping calm.

Mr. Twat is now livid with fury and demands the driver's name, the driver declines to give this information as per company policy but informs Mr. Twat that he only needs to note the time and place if he wishes to complain.

Two minutes had now passed and the bus driver decided it was time to move on; he informed Mr. Twat that he is now leaving, Mr. Twat refuses to get off the bus until the driver gives his name. The driver closes the door and moves off, much to the horror of Mr. Twat.

At the next stop, which was empty, the driver opened the doors to allow Mr. Twat to leave the bus, again Mr. Twat was insistent for the drivers name, the driver closed the doors and drove on, and Mr. Twat now declared that he was being kidnapped. (Short pause to wipe tears away).

Mr. Twat informs the driver that he is going to phone the police, the driver agrees that this would be a very good idea and he would be more than happy to speak to them. During this turn of events, the driver had stopped at every bus stop along the route and opened the doors.

It only takes about four to five minutes to reach the end of the route - the town centre. The driver stops the bus and the passengers alight, along with Mr. Twat whose vocabulary had declined to just a few one and two-syllable words. We know his name was Twat by the way, because someone said it to him as they were leaving. The driver made a written report of the event but no complaint was ever received. I still wonder if he caught a bus back.

It always amazes me that the worst people are respectable, middle-aged men, who if you met socially, would be a fine example of an upright citizen. Who would realise that the very same person, a loving husband, father or grandfather, can let loose a tirade of abuse at some bus driver whilst breaking the law with their illegal parking. It's not just the men; I've met women just as bad.

Here I am: There are instances where the best of intentions go a little awry or are misread. One such instance happened to me in the early days; I caught up with the bus in front that was running very late. As he approached a bus stop with a single customer waiting, he drove straight past. The customer was a little irate to the extent of jumping up and down waving her fist in the air cursing the driver whilst composing a letter of complaint in her mind. How could I tell all this? easy.

In the time it had taken her to raise her fist, I had pulled up beside her, opened the doors and adapted the 'head at a angle' pose. She stood looking at the bus in the distance, she hadn't noticed me and I called out casually "Do you require a bus?" The look on her face was of utter surprise, she almost physically jumped back. Yes, I had combed my hair that morning, "Oh!" was uttered, "I thought . . . . Err."

I explained about the lateness of the other bus and that I was acting as a 'sweeper' and that we only do this if the bus in front knows we're behind them. How she failed to see two identical buses just two bus-lengths apart approaching, I'm not sure but she was now quite happy and a lot wiser. We do these things just for you.

Later on, a smile crossed my face; it was the shortest route, a passenger said: "Do you know driver, your exactly on time.",

"I'm so sorry sir, it won't happen again." Start laughter, he thinking I was joking and me knowing I wasn't.

Bus Groupies: Yes, we have groupies on buses. When I first heard this, I laughed very loudly but that's probably because I'm a bit unstable. My image of groupies are fans that follow their pop idols around the country, getting backstage passes and having wild tea and cake parties as late as nine o'clock in the evening. I might be wrong.

Our Groupies are a little more sedate, almost comatose in some cases. They fall in to two categories - day riders and night riders. The day riders are the commonest by far, always pass-holders of course. They will get on and stay on going round in circles. A few will pick a long distance trip and at the far end will ask you for a ticket back from whence they came. Is it company they seek or just feel the need to be amongst others? They rarely talk to anyone; perhaps it's just the warmth of the bus itself. I personally think it's the nursing homes standing them at bus stops and laying bets as to whether they can find their way back again.

Night riders are a different kettle of fish. This species of groupie prefers the quiet of the evening, always after the rush hour has ceased. They will lurk in shop doorways, watching the buses coming in and judging if there are too many people on-board or whether the driver is one who's friendly towards them - yes they have favourites. These groupies differ from the day riders because they talk and will park themselves near to the driver's seat, sometimes standing behind them. The conversation isn't exciting, often only requiring one word answers but for them it's the rare opportunity to try and hold some sort of conversation with out the feeling of intimidation of other people being there.

There are three regular groupies I have come to know, I seem to draw them like a magnet - must be my natural charm. The one I meet most often is Riff-Raff, a name I have coined for him; he thinks that when I pull up and allow him on I say "Ah, here's the Riff-Raff." meaning 'here's the common man' in a friendly jokey way which always makes him smile. He doesn't know I mean Riff-Raff, as in the character played by Richard O'Brien in the Rocky Horror Show; he's the spitting image of him.

The next character is a woman known as 'Her', as in "Oh god it's her", let's call her 'Unstable Mabel'. It takes a lot of time before Mabel gets comfortable with a driver but when she does, she's latched. Being an inquisitive sort of person, I try to find out a little bit about their background, this is usually when I have a five minute wait at certain timing points on the evening service. Here I can get out of the cab and talk to them face to face rather than a refection on the windscreen. Mabel can be as nice as pie sometimes, giggling at anything you say but other times she feels everything and everyone is wrong and out to upset her. There have been the odd moments when Riff-Raff and she are on the same bus, they hate each other. Riff-Raff won't try to say anything, while she will make sly, derogatory comments, loosely directed at him. It took me a while to learn that she was autistic and has troubles interacting socially.

Character three won't come near me; I call him Hank Marvin because every time I pull up, he disappears into the shadows. Some of the more mature readers amongst you might get that little joke.

Bus Spotters: I knew something was up the moment I rounded the corner in to the bus station. A camera was pointed in my direction from a small group standing on a corner. I parked up and trotted off to find sustenance of the burger kind from the worst McDonald's I've even been in.

Suitably fed up, I set off to walk around the block and happened upon the camera happy group from behind - always an advantage I think. I infiltrated their ranks disguised as a human with a small disadvantage, namely a bus driver's uniform; nonetheless I tried to blend in.

"What do you do with all the pictures then" I said trying to make it sound as if it came from anywhere other than where I was actually standing. "They put them up on the internet" said the small giant standing to my left. "You're Jimmy aren't you?" he added. "!" said me. "We saw you come in, it took a moment to recognise you from the website picture.", "Ah yes, I was a lot younger then." I managed to say. I'd forgotten I put a picture up. Small giant is in fact, the son of a fellow driver from a my area and we knew our paths would cross eventually. I chatted for a short while with the bus spotters asking stupid questions such as: 'How the hell can you tell the difference between makes? They all look the same to me!'

A short time later, two classic buses pulled into the station and a crowd of bus enthusiasts appeared from nowhere and boarded for what I can only assume is a special event trip, and here I am, a bus driver and I knew bugger all about it. I must be moving in the wrong circles again.

Bus spotters are OK; I couldn't eat a whole one, mind you. Once you're aware they exist, you see them everywhere. I did suggest we drivers started up a 'Spot the bus spotter club' but the only club they were interested in was the one they wanted to beat me around the head with.

Oh gosh: There's only one thing that annoys me more than my wife saying 'later' and that's annulled tickets. We all make mistakes, no matter how cautiously we guard against them, we're only human . . . well most bus drivers are. I have my doubts about one guy who likes to eat his lunch out of a bowl on the floor!

Young chap gets on the bus; he's of Afro-Caribbean extraction. I mention this because it does make a difference and I'm crap at impressions. He asks for a ticket, the accent is quite thick and a doubt enters my mind and so I use the standard trick and repeat it back to him. He repeats it again I pause for a moment and hover over the issue button.

"That'll be two pounds sir," he hands over the money, I press the issue button finally. There's a short pause, "it's one pound, twenty." he informs me. Now anyone else would say "No, that's not the right price" when I said two pounds but instead he lets me print the ticket and take the money.

I cancel the ticket and scroll through the fares until I find one that matches one pound, twenty. Nearby this zone, is a street with a name similar to the destination he asked for, my suspicions had been right, hence my delay in issuing the ticket originally.

We deal with many races and accents and we usually get it right in the end but to leave it unquestioned until after the transaction, is very annoying indeed.

I see my favourite group 'Loose Chippings' are appearing in

the next county with two support groups, 'Caution' & 'Soft Verge'.

I'm a bloody idiot (apparently). As I approached a popular bus stop close to town, I see a man getting in to his car that he's parked at the bus stop. I drew up along side and asked the man standing next to the car passenger door: "Is this your car sir?" I enquire. "Yes." replies the aforementioned driver. "You are aware you're parked in a bus stop?" say I. "I'm a window cleaner" he replies. "Oh I do apologise sir, I didn't notice the blue flashing light on top of your car declaring Emergency Window Cleaner On Call sign." Much laughter erupts from within the bus. "You're a bloody idiot." he snarls back. "I don't think so; here comes my second opinion now." I smile.

A second bus pulls in behind me to the stop. People waiting for this bus have to now walk across the front of his car and around by his drivers door to get on the bus behind, one by one they give him a look that only a mother can give to a child who's been very naughty. I had a minute to wait before I could move off and it's amazing how long a minute can last when you're stuck in a car in the wrong place, I knew the driver behind would understand, revenge can be so sweet.

Driver Change-over: "Why do you have to change drivers" asks the first person in the line waiting to get on the bus. I've offered several explanations in the past such as:

I'm not very good at turning left.

I need a wee wee.

My probation officer is waiting for me.

I have to go for my drugs test.

I've just seen someone I ran over last week.

The nursing home says I have to be back by three.

Ken Dodd's dads' dog's dead.

We are allowed breaks. We need to eat, pee and adjust the electronic tag fixed to our leg, only kidding, we don't always pee. I arrived at the changeover point on the sea front, a small line of customers were waiting and the take-over driver stood waiting with a smile - he had bought it earlier from the shop 'round the corner. As I pulled in and lined up with the raised kerb, I opened the door and addressed the waiting throng, "Just changing drivers, won't keep you a moment." however, any group of women wanting to get on a bus has the capability to storm in like a crowd of startled buffalo and one sprightly woman had reached the cab door before I reached the end of the sentence.

"Hospital." she asked

"I'm sorry, we have to change drivers here."

"Can't you just give me a ticket."

"Unfortunately not, I have removed my module and can't issue one now."

"I'll wait here then." she replied.

"I'm sorry, I have to ask you to move off the bus for a moment," I said very politely.

"I'm not moving, I just want a ticket" she argued.

"Madam, I can't issue a ticket and we have to change drivers."

"I'm not moving."

"Madam, I can't leave the bus until you move off."

"I'm not moving." she glared.

"Madam, I can't open the cab door with you standing there, I can't get out."

Silence

"Madam, I can't get out."

More silence very similar to the first, they might even be related.

"Madam, I need to open the cab door." I wasn't going to give in, I was genuinely trapped. It took another three attempts to get out of the cab. I resorted to opening the cab door until it rested against her, swivelled in the seat facing her and tossed my bag down on the floor over her shoulder.

Only then did she shuffle slightly to one side. I slid out, smiled at the other driver, no words were needed and walked off, with the crowd looking daggers at her. Still, it gave them something to talk about on the trip and no-doubt loud enough for her to hear. How to avoid driver change over - get on at the stop around the corner.

Mufti day: All drivers and staff could dress down or get in to some sort of fancy dress. All for charity I should add, some really don't need a reason.

Did I join in this event you are thinking; well I have to admit I didn't, so why not? My shift that day was the first bus out at

05:25am and as I got up at 04:30 that morning a dread thought crossed my mind, what if I had got the day wrong and turned up as say Joan of Arc only to discover my error and had no time to go home and change? I think I needed the reassurance of seeing other drivers dressed up first and that won't happen if I'm the first out.

I made the excuse that I was going to come in to work as a Dalek but had trouble stepping up onto the bus. Yes I know they are fitted with ramps but have you ever seen a Dalek bend down to unfold a ramp? Plus of course, steering would have been a problem, and not to mention finishing each sentence with "EX-TER-MIN-ATE' regardless of how appropriate it may be!

Instead, I went dressed as a professional bus driver, no, don't laugh and enjoyed spotting other drivers. I loved one dressed as a vicar; I would have finished each sentence with 'bless you' and splashed them with holy water (Avian or Volvic). Another chap I met in the rest room was dressed as a schoolboy complete with stick on scabs and catapult, we should do this more often, I have some of my wife's underwear set aside.

Chapter thirteen: Spare & bus rallies.

And then three come along at once. No, not buses, BUS STOPS! It has amused me for some time now, that there is one area on my route that has three bus stops very close together, in fact, there is a point where you can see all three at once. Welcome to the Cemetery Roundabout! I should hasten to add, that it is the council that own and place the bus stops and not bus companies.

Bus stop one, is a new stop that has been placed adjacent to a new housing estate that has recently been built. It has a lovely new shelter, complete with a timetable board mounted inside. Before this bus stop came in to existence, there were, and still are, bus stops each side less than 300 yards away, Still, what's a few thousand pounds of taxpayers money for a short path, railings and a traffic island?

I'm spare: Monday and I was 'Spare' and so was required to hang around the depot waiting for a driver to go ill, not turn up, lose a bus, get one wedged in a tunnel, get lost or storm into the office shouting that they've had enough - The customers were being far too nice to him.

Now many may think this is a bit of an easy number, I know I did, but I can assure you that after 30 minutes you soon get bored, having read every notice on the wall. I soon realised that if you need a notice to be read by everyone, just stick it next to the clock.

An hour later and I've carbon dated the sandwiches in the vending machine, tried all 7 versions of coffee on offer, strolled to the toilet twice, (side effect of coffee), tried to corner a seagull in the car park and waved at a passing airplane.

By the forth hour, I've split the atom using just a piece of flint and a sponge, learnt how to do a trick with an elastic band that didn't involve body parts, disproved Einstein's theory of relativity, shaved off all my body hair and made a nice tea cosy out of it and written a book. To write a book, get a piece of paper and a pen and write 'A Book' on it.

Time for a break I thought and scurried off to KFC for some

unidentifiable lumps of greasy chicken in a leaky box. Why do they put more paper towels and lemon finger wipes in the box than there are pieces of chicken? I sit in the car to devour my feast whilst having an audience of a lone seagull perched on the bonnet watching me with its white eyes. I mused for a while why they still have webbed feet, these buggers never go near the water any more.

In the afternoon, a job came up - it was my favourite countryside run; this was too good to be true. It was. The journey up was uneventful and very quiet I sang most of the way. Pulling in to the turn around point at the far end, I got out for my 10 minute waiting time, lit a fag and waved at the yokels.

10 minutes up, I got back in and checked my running board. There must be some sort of mistake; it says I'm here for half an hour and that can't be right. I rechecked and even asked a passer-by who looked like they could read. Yes confirmed, I had another twenty minutes.

Within 10 minutes, a flotilla of buses arrived. Yes, I know flotilla the wrong word but what else can you call a collection of buses? Suggestions please.

Every type of public transport turned up - buses, coaches, mini-buses and a bloke with a wheelbarrow - this is the countryside you know. I started to wonder if this was the place buses came to die. It turned out to be the school run. I'd been tricked.

The normally quiet bus stop was suddenly transformed to a crowd scene on a hot August day in Trafalgar Square - they swarmed hither and thither like an exploded centipede. 'Golly gosh' I said to myself, or words to that effect. It turned out not to be quite that bad, only about half a dozen were going my way, plus a few 'normals'.

The school runs in town can be a nightmare but out here it was so different, the children were polite and well-behaved, the sheep were a problem but nothing I couldn't sort out with a broom.

What the Dickens? Driving in a well known city port one morning, I couldn't help but notice a bus shelter marked with the words 'Birthplace of Charles Dickens' and I thought to myself that his mother mush have been caught short on the way back from Bingo that night.

Sweet revenge: I approached the bus stop and my heart did a little whoop of joy, for there before me, was a taxi. I would have rubbed my hands together with glee but the shop had sold out. Now this stop always has a car parked just before it, making it a difficult one to pull into correctly but I managed to squeeze in, with the front of the bus inches from the rear bumper of the taxi that was parked at the other end.

Passengers loaded, I was ready to go when suddenly, I notice before me a taxi. My goodness, how did that get there, I said to myself, leaning on the horn. The driver stuck his head out of the window (I use the term 'driver' loosely here). "Sorry mate, can't move, I've broken down." he said. "What, mentally or physically?" I enquired. "Eh." was his best reply; I don't think he got it. "Oh dear," I said, "You'll have to see me out whilst I reverse then."

I had a feeling the breakdown was a ploy and so I was going to make him suffer. Did I mention it was pouring with rain?

Had a bit of a fright the other day down a country lane, no, don't get excited, it wasn't a flasher. I rounded a bend in my 'Decker', only to see an articulated lorry just about to come out of a side road. Now the driver had approached the junction and slowed but was fully expecting to pull straight out without stopping. The only reason he did stop, was the surprise of seeing a double Decker bearing down on him and the inability he had of steering with one hand whilst he ate a sandwich with the other. I think his digestive tract might have sped up a bit, by the look on his face. I am so pleased our buses are fitted with cameras.

A well known bus company started an advertising campaign. The graphics were in the form of a garden washing line with clothing pegged up, with me so far? Each item had a letter on the front, these being: M.T.W.T.F.S.S. It was promoting a seven day ticket. This 'ad' was wrapped around the bus but this meant only W.T.F. was on display on the rear end. We all know WTF is text speak for What The F***.

Girl's girl's girls: One night, as I neared the end of a late shift and was parked on the seafront, not literally, I detected the sound that puts a smile on many a bus driver's face. A group of tipsy young ladies, fresh from a local club or pub that must have been holding a Vicars and Tarts party, were dressed appropriately, if that's the right word, in little more than stockings, suspenders and bosom-thrusting Basques.

Unlike a group of drunken lads, tipsy young ladies are not often problematic, (today's long word) and these were no exception.

I had three people on the bus, two elderly and one middle aged and I thought, should I close the door to save their blushes in case the passing language was ripe, or should I stand in the doorway giving my 'I'm in charge here, behave yourselves' look but then realised that this would, in fact, make me a target and so instead I remained sat down, holding up my running board, trying to look disinterested, occasionally peeping over the top - did I mention the suspenders?

I needn't have worried. They passed by in the cheerful throng that they were, except for the last one who paused as she drew level with the door. "Are you In Service tiger? . . . Grrrr" she said, winked and carried on by. I took that memory home with me.

Another day: "Of course I can change a 10 pound note sir." replied I, trying not to burst a blood vessel. I waved goodbye to the last of my change. "Sorry about that." he says, as he goes off to find his seat. "No need to apologise sir, it's me that the next customer will be blaming when I start handing out change vouchers." lucky, I forgot to say it out loud. Honestly, a tenner for such a small fare, I have that sort of loose change down the back of my sofa.

"How much is a city return?" asked the man who had not found the word 'please' in the dictionary. "£6.00 sir" I replied touching my forelock (My wife likes me to do that). "£6.00" he replies, "That's too much."

A long pause followed and was joined by another. I'm not quite sure what he expected me to do about it, perhaps I should have made him an offer, say perhaps he could travel free on the roof of the bus or he could run alongside for a while. "£6.00." he said again, "Yes sir." Pause number three slid into place. Whilst he stood there gazing at me, I checked off the rest of the customers and began unwrapping pause number four when he turned and left the bus. I closed the doors, happy in the knowledge that he couldn't find a cheaper option, now that Uncle Toms Flying Carpet Emporium had closed down.

Special thanks to 'Big John', as he likes to be known, except on the weekends when he prefers to be called Mary. I had just set up a bus I had taken over and pulled up to the waiting hoards, sun glinting off their silver hair and the smell of primrose oil filled the air. As I tried to key in the destination number for the first customer, the ticket machine rejected it. I tried again and again, panic started to raise its head. "My apologies ladies and gentlemen, I seem to be having a malfunction."

It was one of those moments when you scan the crowd for a friendly face and my eye caught sight of John pulling up on the opposite side of the road. Keeping my composure, I ran screaming across the road and threw myself on his mercy, which fortunately he had already fluffed-up for me.

I explained my problems and he recommended some cream to rub on, then I asked him about the ticket machine. He gave a couple of knowledgeable nods (he would normally charge for these) and hopped out of his cab, did I mention he was wearing a bunny costume? He watched me reset the machine and immediately spotted my mistake, a wrong number . . . time to blush I think, one of those silly mistakes that made me feel like I was a fresh-faced-just-passed-my-test trainee. John smiled and pointed out which direction I should go when I left the stop, just in case. I guess that's a coffee then.

I came back: What possesses me to drive something the size of a small house down a crowded street? This is one of the thoughts going through my head as I climb back in the cab after a week off. Thank goodness for panty-liners, that's all I can say.

A sunny, warm July day saw me setting off to the city, which to me is like trying to run from one end of Marks and Spencer's to the other on a half-price sales day. One thing that does amuse me however, are the local city buses - they all have names. Each bus carries the name of a famous city resident, be they actor, writer or maybe murderer. We, at our depot, were thinking of doing the same thing; so far we've come up with, Sleepy, Dopey and Grumpy.

I've been waiting for this to happen and today it did. I approached a Railway Station and was fortunately driving a bus, just ahead are some traffic lights with a selection of three colours. Red being the most popular - people stop to admire it, and green being the least liked, people drive past it. Amber is liked by some but comes a close second to the green.

Anyway, ahead at the lights (red), was a line of cars and I joined on the end of this line, as it just happened to be right next to the bus stop and a passenger wanted to get off. Now what I enjoyed was that this was a rare moment when I could stop and still be in the line of traffic and let a passenger off and not have to indicate that I was going to pull in to the side of the road.

Passenger alighted, (got off, not set fire to), and doors closed, I sat and waited for the lights to change. Meanwhile, one car driver assumed I was at the bus stop - remember I wasn't indicating that, and drove around me to find the gap between me and the car in front was about three feet, deep joy. I looked down into the car. The driver now positioned smack in the middle of the road next to me, was a tad embarrassed, I smiled, he avoided looking at me, and then another car tried exactly the same thing.

The lights changed and we started to move off. Did they now, somewhat humbled with their display of bad driving, wait for me to get out of the way? No, both decided to zoom off and cut across the front of me. I assume, to bury their collective heads in the sand somewhere. I enjoyed it.

Bus Rally: I am not a bus spotter or an anorak honest. I drive the things and so I have a natural interest, that's all there is to it. Understand that I do not get excited about photos of buses, I just happen to take 200, and anyway, my finger slipped most of the time . . . and . . . and. . .

Strangely enough, these were the phrases that not only I uttered to anyone who asked, but certain 'off duty' bus drivers I know who just happened to be there said the same thing.

And so the Bus Rally came to town, which was a bit of luck because that's what was printed on the posters so it must have been intentional then. There were about 70 buses of all shapes and sizes, and about 50 times as many enthusiasts to go along with them. As each entrant came around the corner, it was accompanied by the combined zoom-click of a thousand camera shutters and a hundred pens scribbling in notebooks, 'Ah, DFG 510, not seen that since 98, same chassis but up to four body types,' whilst the passing general public limited it down to 'There's a red one'.

What did surprise me, was the numbers of stalls along the seafront that were selling bus related items and by this I mean model buses, old timetables, black and white photographs, videos, posters and framed prints, there's a whole support industry behind all this. It's bus porn!

And so my conclusion is, as long as these people don't start writing about it on the internet because then I would worry . . . ah . . . scrap that.

Gotcha! "Child single to Ashbourne Drive please." asks the young man. "I'm sorry, I can't do a child single.", "Oh, why's that?" he asks. "Because I was watching you swigging from a lager can as I approached, so you must be 18.", "Oh well, it was worth a try."

Pop goes the weasel (or squirrel): This is a sad story, so if you like cute furry creatures, then DO NOT READ ANY FURTHER.

I know you're going to but don't say I didn't warn you. OK. Nice day, early morning and about halfway along my route just passing through the local villages, when I see a squirrel in the road ahead of me.

Normally I would slow down a bit to allow it time to run off, as they always do, and as I drew closer, it did the 'Trapped-in-the-headlights' thing. It started to try to go one way and then the other but without actually moving from the same spot in the road.

Now with only a few feet to go, I saw what the problem was, it's back end had been run over and squashed into the ground. Its head, forearms and upper-torso were still mobile and scrambling for a direction to go in. I ran over it.

In the few microseconds I had to think about it, I knew its time was limited. If I didn't get it, the next car might. I could see it was beyond rescue, you can take a lot in graphically in a second or two. With a minor deviation to my line of travel, I ensured the front wheel did what was required.

I won't explain the sound that followed or the image that went through my mind but it was not pleasant at all.

Why are you late driver : Sitting on the promenade, watching small children throwing stones at passing mobility scooters, may sound the ideal way to pass a summer's afternoon, and so it should be, this is what summer is all about, but my mind is focused on one thing, where's the bloody bus? I'm due to take over a bus that's already 10 minutes late. I have my bucket and spade at the ready, knotted hanky on my head and ice cream stains down my shirt, I just need a bus. I spot my old bus driving instructor on the sea front. By old, I mean the bus we learnt on was old, not the instructor. "Hello Rod, what are you up to?" I ask, by way of conversation. "Doing driving assessments." a wicked smile crossed his face. "Ah." say I, inwardly panicking. "Where are you off to?" he asks. "The city.", "Oh, I think I'll stick to something a bit more local." he says and wanders off to find another victim. Phew! Both he and I knew he would end up miles away from the depot, his car and his dinner.

Eventually the bus turns up, not the drivers fault - Knowing the passion our councils have for digging up roads and installing temporary traffic lights that give equal time to each road, even that side road that nothing comes out of.

After a brief exchange of knitting patterns and bodily fluid with the driver (just kidding), I set off at last just 12 minutes down, not too bad, should be able to make that up. I know the bus ahead of me was late too and hopefully that he would be picking up my passengers ahead of me and I'll have a chance to catch up and get back on time . . . well that was the plan.

A couple of miles further on and the other bus could only have left the stop I was approaching a few minutes ahead of me but already there was a small crowd gathered, placards in hand declaring 'We want Jimmy' I pull in and load up. Now 15 minutes down, I eventually trundle off in the general direction of 'away'.

'Bloody gates' a common curse of bus drivers after 'Bloody

people': The crossings were down and there before me, a line of half a dozen and a mobility scooter. I'm sat there in line, the gates go up, deep joy, and then they go down again. Only a couple of cars got across, having slowed by the mobility scooter. This section of road had no pavements, the whole public transport system brought to a crawl by something that was the mutated offspring of a Dalek.

I didn't make it, naturally. I use the time to finish off my colouring book and the gates eventually go up and I'm off again. Eventually, I get to the next town some 20 minutes down. "Why are you so late driver?" asks the first to board, "it took another 12 minutes to clean up the blood and hide the body".

What: "A Concessionary Day-Rover City Rider please' asked the nice gentleman. I replied with a '!' - which is a raised eyebrow for those that don't know me. Somehow, this bloke had managed to create a new ticket from three other types. I love it when this happens, you have to turn detective. A polite enquiry as to how much it had cost him last time and I ran through the ticket options until I found a matching price and he was happy. What happened to the other six dwarfs I don't know.

Later that very day, I was 'resting' on a bench on the forecourt of a bus station with my colouring book when this little scenario unfolded before me. A local bus pulled in to the stop nose-first, like many bus stations it's nose in, arse out. The bus stopped, always a good idea, the doors opened, will these good ideas never end, and the passengers got off.

The bus remained there, mouth-open for another three or so minutes until it was time to leave. The driver closed the doors, as this stops people falling out. He then engaged reverse gear and checked behind. My attention was broken by the clatter of someone trying to run in high heels, I look 'round to see if it was my slightly eccentric uncle Richard, only to see a woman who started shouting "Stop, stop" to the bus driver who couldn't hear her.

She got close enough to bang on the windscreen of the bus as it started to pull out, but the driver carried on his reversing manoeuvre. Now you may think, 'bastard' as many do but once the doors are closed and the bus is signalling (reversing lights and horn) it is 'committed to go'. It's not just company policy, it's an insurance requirement. You won't win a claim if they can prove the bus was clearly signalling and in a manoeuvre when the passenger chased after it. What made it worse, was that she stood there and in a loud voice declared "You've made me late."

Strange, the bus left on time and she was late, not the bus. No-doubt when she got to work, she would relate a story of a rude, ignorant bus driver who made her late, not the real fact that it was her error.

On the other side of the coin however, if the driver has not signalled and it is safe to do so, he will generally open the doors, it's his responsibility and one that's not taken lightly. OK, rant over.

It's a fair cop: It started like every other day, the earth rotates, the sun shines past bits of old Apollo rocket engines, gently illuminating the haze over the sewage works. Oh if only Constable were alive today, what a picture he'd paint . . . or scratch.

Expecting the usual run-of-the-mill stuff, I got excited when I approached a stop on the way to town. A little old lady was stood beside a police officer waiting for my bus. My mind was racing ahead, had she been dealing in black-market mothballs or perhaps a stolen recipe for a Victorian sponge but alas it was just a coincidence. Pity.

As I closed in on the bus stop, a lady 'Of a certain age' pulled into the stop from the opposite side of the road. I honked my horn and mouthed the words 'You can't park there', or words that conveyed a similar meaning - she chose to ignore me. I opened the door while the nice, uniformed policeman spoke to her.

She got quite animated, he explained the simple 'You just can't stop in a bus stop' rule in some detail and got on the bus, informing me that 'Some action' would be taken and closed his notebook. I thanked him for taking 'Some action' on this all too common problem and then asked him if he wanted to also speak to the driver of the car behind that had just pulled into the bus stop behind me.

Off he went, polishing his whistle - bless him. The car driver, on seeing the nice policeman, decided to leave. My day was looking up.

A little later on, a different bus and route took me into a supermarket car park. Well, almost. As I came up the access road, a blur of grey with a touch of blue rinse shot across the front of the bus and buried itself in to the bushes at the side of the road . . . and a tree.

Some very frail old lady had decided to cut a new road, rather than follow the accustomed tarmac route. I stopped the bus, hazards flashing, engine off and went off to see if I could interest her in some life-insurance. She was alright, shaken and confused but OK. The tissue box on the back shelf had become dislodged but wasn't an immediate danger. We left her in the car while I phoned an ambulance until a small fire started at the front of the car. Not the large blazing-inferno it will become each time I re-tell the story later back at the yard.

We removed her from the car and as luck would have it, two fire engines were in the car park on some promotional work, handing out matches to children - one came over and the professionals took over.

I directed traffic because I had a nice day-glow vest until the ambulance turned up and then buggered off. On my return to the depot, brimming over with wanting to relate the story, the controllers already knew, how annoying is that? The police had contacted them because the bus I was driving has cameras all over it and the whole scene caught on tape or hard drive. I just hope they don't see the bit where I'm going through her handbag.

To round off the day, I was required to see the boss on an unrelated event. It would appear that there are things called 'Mystery Shoppers' who go around checking things like what bus drivers are like whilst posing as a passenger. Oh dear, I'm for it I can tell!

It turns out, I was caught on a good day and did well-enough to be thanked for it. Money would have been nice . . . No seriously, just being thanked can make a big difference. Just this very morning, the first three passengers that boarded were greeted with a 'Good morning' by me and I received not a word of reply, just weekly passes shoved in my face. Yes, it's a funny day . . . mostly.

Chapter fourteen: Acronyms

I pull in to a bus stop to let customers off after I've had enough of their screaming, it's common practice to glance at the internal mirror, then see them rise out of their seats, ready to leave. My mind makes a mental note of how many are leaving and I do a bit of knitting whilst I wait. But hang on, I saw at least half a dozen, that's 6 pre-metric, get up but only two have passed me on the way out. A look in the mirror reveals all are sitting down. It turns out that the general public, in confined spaces, like to play musical chairs.

We bus drivers have a sort of collection of acronyms we use to describe people when talking within earshot of the general public, it goes a little like this:

OFA: Over-Friendly Alcoholic.
Found loitering around bus shelters, rarely seen in daylight, often surrounded by a blue haze. Generally not dangerous but try not to breathe in. Avoid any physical contact, even if they insist on shaking your hand and telling you how much they love you.
FOB: Fragile Old Bird/Bloke.
Deceptive this one, often has small wheeled shopping basket in tow, makes a considerable effort to get on the bus but can lift the shopping trolley on with one hand. Will often ask to go to the place they have just got on at then slap your arm and say "Silly me, what am I thinking." Usually harmless but can be armed with walking stick which will fall to the floor at least once during the journey. Can take a while to select a suitable seat. Will give you a sweet on leaving the bus. So far I've had boiled sweets, a plum, a pork pie, several packets of crisps and a small box of chocolates. I have declined one offer of being their 'toy boy' on one occasion.
TSP: Two Stick Pensioners.
As above, plus – Considerably fragile, can get entangled with the handrails, will drop walking stick whilst looking for their free pass. Always wait until they have sat down and fallen

asleep before moving off. On exit, wait until they have moved away from the doors, as the draught from them closing can knock them over.

BIFF: Bloke in Flip-Flops.

Old Hippy, may have braided hair and beads around their wrist and addresses you as 'Man'.

D&C

Dazed and confused. Gets on the bus thinking it's the Mobile Library.

DOUBLE H: Harried Housewife.

Not found at bus shelters but rather running towards one, often with carrier bags in both hands. Whilst she puts down the bags and is searching for her purse uttering "It's here somewhere, I know it.", make sure to quickly hand her the ticket before she picks up the bags again.

GOG: Go on, Guess.

Fairly common, will board the bus and show pass but not actually speak or acknowledge your kindly welcome. Will assume you are related to Uri Geller and know where they are going.

TRD: Ticket Roll Destroyer.

Just has the knack of pulling most of the ticket roll out of the machine. Has been known, in one instance, to have actually walked the length of the bus before it eventually snapped.

NP: No problems.

Customers have the right money, use the correct pass at the right time, will return your welcome, will sit in the nearest seats and press the stop button in plenty of time. Usually happens in months ending in a P.

And last but not least, a donation from Charles in the USA.

LOUT: Loud Obnoxious Urban Teen. Easily distinguishable by the tinny buzzing of their ear buds being played at a level guaranteed to turn their brains to jelly. They usually yell to make sure you can hear them above the music (the term "music" is used very loosely). Often oblivious to their surroundings and tend towards outbursts of off-key singing and air guitar.

There are a few more but the number of F's involved gets a little embarrassing.

Making a pass: "I'm sorry, your pass is out of date." says the kindly bus driver (me). "Oh, what can I do?" asks the perplexed woman. "Apply to the council for a new one, meanwhile you'll have to pay for your ticket I'm afraid." answers the Adonis-like driver (Shut up, I can dream).

Flicking back my golden locks in slow motion, like the bird on the shampoo advert, I slide out the old pass from its wallet and what does it reveal? . . . yet another pass underneath and another and another. In fact, six of the things going back to 2001 and low and behold . . . a new one!

I look at her with my blue eyes (that bit's true); raising an eyebrow in a quizzical fashion, Roger Moore, you'd be proud of me. She looks at me and goes a bit weak, I have that effect, and releases a small giggle, we are allowed to carry small animals on the buses. "Oh, is that the new one then?" she asks. "Yes, I smile, where you like would to go?" Bess her.

Two in ten minutes: "A written ticket to own." said the Indian woman when I asked her for the destination. Hmm thought I, perhaps she was just visiting our country and wanted a bus ticket signed by me to show off to her family back in New Delhi. After we both threw the phrase around for a while, we eventfully settled for 'A return ticket to town'.

"I don't know what the road's called but there's a dentist on the corner." said the elderly gentleman. Well, this narrowed it down a bit. I started to name a couple of nearby bus stops. "No, that's too far" he said "Would you recognise it if you saw it?" I asked. "Oh yes, there's a dentist on the corner".

Getting the feeling I had jumped in to a Monty Python sketch, I had to break the chain that was forming - after all, dementia may be catching. "How about I give you a ticket to the next main bus stop and if you spot it on the way, just ring the bell" I said . . . hopefully. His mouth opened to speak or it could have just been the weight of his bottom denture but I managed to run off a concessionary ticket and hand it to him and in the same movement, addressed the customer waiting behind him breaking his monopoly on me.

It was two stops along, one stop before the main one I had ticketed him for. There was a tiny brass plate on the gate of the corner house, declaring . . . chiropodist.

Sholley: The personal four-wheeled shopping tolley. I think I speak for many bus drivers when I say that the sight of these four by four pensioner specials makes you curse the day the wheel was invented, and where would we have been if someone hadn't invented the axle I ask you? Lets look at the plus-points of these Sholley's shall we . . . there, that didn't take long, did it?

These things have three times the capacity of the much smaller two wheeled version, if they were to fill one up, which they don't, they wouldn't be able to move it, let alone get one on a bus. Unlike the soft bodied two wheeler, these have a skin scrapping metal cage surround, resembling an oversized, square waste paper basket.

The four wheels are fixed, as in, they don't steer at all, but worst of all, they don't fit in the bus. Oh yes, they can get them on and then proceed to park them in the wheelchair – baby buggy space. I'm not sure what to do if a wheelchair or large baby buggy were to try to board the bus. Do I refuse a mother or wheelchair bound person to travel because there's some shopping in the way or get them to move them out and block the aisles, which is a big no-no, just in case someone at the back of the bus self-combusts.

Can't win, won't win : I was approaching a bus stop in stealth mode - lights off and the word 'Truck' written on a piece of card in the window, when I saw people at a bus stop trying to get my attention, so I pulled in. At the back of the small crowd was . . . a motorised wheelchair.

Being the thoughtful driver I am, I slid the bus up to the raised kerb perfectly, tiny slivers of aluminium peeling off the step edge, (it was that perfect) and lowered the front suspension with a satisfying 'pshhhhhhhhhhhh'.

"I need the ramp down." said the motorised wheelchair. "I think you'll find it's perfectly level." I smiled. "I need the ramp down." she repeats. "You can do that, he's got it just right." said a bystander. "I need the ramp down." Needless to say, I got the ramp out. I had to move the bus forward to clear the bus stop sign, raise the suspension, put it in neutral, turn the engine off, climb out, unfold the ramp and stand behind her as she buzzed up.

I don't mind doing the ramp, in most cases wheelchair users are very adept at getting on and off with no help whatsoever but when the local council spends thousands of pounds building raised kerbs and the bus company spends millions getting 'low floor buses' and the two meet in the middle perfectly, it does annoy me when someone insists on using something that isn't required. In fact, it made it worse, but the customer is always right. Funny how she didn't need the ramp to get off!

New hobby: Punting. No, not floating idyllically down an Oxford river wearing a straw boater and blazer with my pole in my hand but the art of pushing vehicles out of bus stops. On a normal day, (insert maniacal laughter) I'll meet at least two 'punts' parked up, blocking bus stops.

My usual technique is to pull up right behind them and honk them out of the way, the waiting customers love this. The other technique is the 'Punt Block'. This is where the bus is driven across the front of the vehicle at an angle, this emphasises just how much they are in the way, the back end of the bus will still be out in the road but the cars behind can clearly see that I can't get into the bus stop.

The last technique is parallel parking where you can only park up level but still in the road. This, blocks the road completely; it prevents the 'Punt' from driving off, or in many cases, even getting back in their car.

The sad thing about these punts is, they are nearly always mature drivers, not yobs or boy-racers but Mr and Mrs Average who can't be bothered to park properly to post a letter or go to a cash machine. Are they doing any harm? Well yes they are, it forces passengers to walk out in the road, causes problems for any 'wheeled' objects to enter the bus and makes a problem for the less-able if we can't draw up to the kerb and of course, it's a Traffic Offence. Out of interest, I looked up satellite pictures of my favourite 'punting' spots and every picture has a car at the bus stop.

It's been an uneventful week so far, I did think that I had developed the Black Death Plague for a while but it turned out to be a sultana stuck on my arm. Got a new vending machine in the rest room, simple to use. Button one equals coffee, button two equals coffee with cup.

Christmas is just around the corner and the goose is getting fat, which is a shame as we all tend to eat turkey these days. The council has dusted off its coloured light bulb in readiness for the festive season and has placed homeless people on every street corner, should you feel the need to adopt one over the festive period. I'm given to understand, a mince pie is to be included. Remember, this is a time for giving and the right change is a good place to start.

There will be no bus service on Christmas day, we can't fit them in the church, but there will be an invisible one on Boxing Day so I wouldn't bother to leave the house if I were you. Normal service is resumed on the 27th of December, assuming the mixture of drunks and reindeer droppings have been swept up. You do still believe don't you?

Yes I am being a bit flippant I know. Christmas has become so plastic and tacky now, driven by commercialism and corporate greed - we all know it's just the run up to a New Years Sales drive, the true spirit of Christmas is in people, not objects. So give your neighbour a hug . . . and that cheap aftershave your in-laws bought you.

On the subject of giving, I gave myself an early present. Being a bit of a beer-fan with a leaning towards real ale, for 'leaning' read 'falling over', I purchased a home brew kit to play with. 40 pints of Porter should be ready in the New Year, which will make me a very happy bunny indeed.

Will Smith I hate you: You may be familiar with Mr. Smith, the film star person. His latest film at the time I originally wrote this was Legend. The supporting adverting poster campaign, shows Mr. Smith almost full size. These posters were emblazoned bus stops all over the country.

I've lost count how many times I've stopped at an empty bus stop at night because this bloody poster is on display. From a distance, it looks like someone waiting at the stop, so I pull in and there he is, all smug and laughing at me.

Down and outs in suburbia. We've all seen them, slumped in alleyways, propping up telephone boxes, lying forlornly in hedgerows across the country, desolate, unloved, needy, stripped of their past and no future to look forward to. No, I'm not talking of tramps and drunks, I'm talking about discarded Christmas trees.

Chapter fifteen: Getting on a bus, the guide.

The Drunk: Couldn't believe I actually got away with this one. It was dark; I slid the bus up to the bus stop, hoping the swaying punter standing there didn't see me. To add to the illusion, I whistled tunelessly, trying to imitate an ice cream van. He lurched in my direction like a puppet with half the strings cut. He raised a leg up, to climb the step – I lowered the step at the same speed he put his foot down hoping for an amusing incident and failed. "Where would you like to go sir?" I asked, adding a slight Italian accent just in case the Ice Cream rouse was working and he asked for a 'Mr Whippy with chocolate chips'. "I'd like to go home pleeeesh." he answered with a lopsided smile. I paused momentarily . . . "Well, here we are sir."

He turned on the spot and stepped off. "Cheers mate." he said and wandered in a general 'away' direction. I closed the doors and joined the traffic. Had it really been that easy? Yes.

Magnetic qualities of bus stop poles. The council owns the bus stops as you already know. They make it 40 foot in length to fit a bus in. With me so far? . . . good, I shall continue. Where do they often stick the post, at the very beginning? Where do people queue up? . . . at the post, where are the doors on a bus . . . at the other end. We call it the front.

Now is the winter of our discotheque (stupid spell-checker). Readers of the Daily Mail on the 22nd of January, would have noticed an article entitled 'How to get on a bus – the idiots guide to travelling from A to B', I've decided to update it:

First and foremost, it is important to recognise that a bus, unlike taxi's, don't have the word BUS written on the front. If you find yourself travelling and see the word TESCO upside-down, then chances are you're in a shopping trolley, try again.

If you see a queue of people, join it, there may be a bus at the other end. Buses do NOT have blue flashing lights. If it has a red light on one side and a green light on the other, then you're on a ship. The best place to find a bus, is amongst a crowd of elderly people holding special white cards - buses are attracted to these cards.

A bus makes a 'putshuuuush' noise when it stops, as do trucks. If you have to raise your leg over waist height to get on and the driver's wearing a checked shirt, it's a lorry - say sorry and admire his Yorkie bar for a moment before departing.

Buses have an illuminated sign at the front, this is its destination. 'Sorry – Not in Service' is NOT a destination, it means the driver is very shy and finds it hard to mix with people.

When a bus pulls up, wait for it to stop before trying to get on, otherwise you'll get a nasty friction-burn on your face. After a short period, the doors will open.

The driver will be the person usually sitting at the front, holding the steering wheel. If there is no steering wheel, you're on a train.

When you get on, tell the driver where you want to go - just the name of the town or area is enough. Saying things like '23 Lofthouse Road' will result in the driver pointing to a taxi. Bus drivers are highly trained but mind-reading is a skill yet to be acquired, so don't forget to move your mouth when talking to him/her.

There are two basic types of tickets, single or return. You can be married and still buy a single. If you ask for a return ticket, the driver will ask "Where to?" Do not answer – "Back here of course" because it's an old joke that's wearing very thin.

There have been many advances in technology in the last few years and most buses are now fitted with seats (except school buses, which have cages). Make your way down the bus, to allow other people to get on. If you find yourself back outside, then you've gone too far.

After a while, the doors will close and the bus start to move forward (most of the time). Do not panic and try not to shout out "Oh my god, we're all going to die" as it can unsettle the other passengers.

You are permitted to shout "Wheeeee" if the bus goes down a hill. When you get to the area you want, or just want to get off to pick some flowers, press the red button situated on the many metal posts holding the roof up - JUST ONCE. Do not try to climb out of the windows, but wait until it comes to a halt (this is when the scenery outside stops moving), the nice driver will open the doors for you, thank the driver and give him any gold-coloured coins you may have, for safe-keeping. Tea and biscuits are not served on a bus.

Many first time passengers find the excitement too much and forget to keep breathing and fall over. All bus drivers are trained in dragging limp bodies off a bus. Bus tickets can help as part of a calorie-controlled diet but it does make it difficult should the inspector get on. We look forward to meeting you.

Chapter sixteen: Funny things people.

Had another drunk on the bus the other day. Well, almost. As the passengers got on, one chap leaned over (I thought he was going to kiss me for a moment) and whispered "You don't want to let that bloke on mate" Now normally drunks aren't much of a problem, I charge them £20 and they seem quite happy when I tell them the bar's at the back - just open the little door there marked 'Emergency Exit', but this one was different. "Where do you want to go to sir?" I asked, hoping I could tell him this was the wrong bus but no, he knew where he was going and waved his free pass at me. "I'm sorry sir, but I don't think I should allow you to travel on this bus", "I'm not getting off" he replied. He had placed himself on the front platform and was leaning on the open door, I was tempted to close the doors but remembered that rather than force him out, they would force him in.

Now the battle of wills began. I knew all eyes were upon me. The passengers all had faces that showed concern and they were in agreement with me but they wanted a show. Where else could you be entertained for just £1.25? As I climbed out of the driving seat, I glanced at the passengers and to a man, they looked away and took great interest in the posters on the bus. I could faintly hear the opening bars of 'The Good, The Bad and The Ugly' playing in the wind and the sound of spurs. "If you don't get off my bus, I'm going to . . . look a right idiot" was the thought going through my mind. "I'm sorry sir, but I consider you to be a risk to the bus, its passengers and to yourself and for that reason, I must insist you leave the bus." I said, in my best authoritative tone. "No." was the simple reply. I did have an ace up my sleeve but I was saving that for a game of poker later.

I stepped off the bus (I had turned the engine off just in case he got a silly idea) and phoned the depot for advice - they suggested calling the police. "I'm going to have to call the police and have you removed.", I informed him, waving my mobile phone around pretending it was a light sabre like in Star Wars - I was even doing the sound effects!

He got off. I got on the bus and apologised to the passengers for the delay and drove off into the sunset, Sainsbury's actually. I kept a straight face but the sense of relief was massive. One passenger complimented me on my handling of the situation. My fear was that this man would fall over on someone or just throw up; both would put the bus out of commission and ruin my day. Now is the time to say a big thank you to the unsung heroes in the bus depots, the cleaners, I've seen what they have had to deal with and it isn't pretty.

Sunday Bloody Sunday: You'd think Sunday would be an easy shift, well I did for a while until I tried to squeeze past the repenter's cars stacked up outside the churches. Christians they may be, law-abider's they're not! Perhaps the church had a special offer on that Sunday: Two sins for the price of one.

A Bit of a Moan: The evening ended well I thought, the town was the end of the line and the end of my shift. As I drove in to the high street, I discovered a car just pulling into the bus stop outside KFC. I beeped my horn, they got out, looked at me and walked off in to KFC. I parked my bus across the front of it. It wasn't so much that they were in the way, illegally parked or just pig- ignorant but to add insult to injury, they had entered a pedestrian-only area, no cars permitted. Now I needed an excuse to sit there for a few minutes and hope one of our super-efficient wardens to appear . . . my excuse arrived.

The next stop would be the depot and so I used the time to gather my things together, shark repellent, spear gun, CS spray and had just finished mopping up the blood off the floor, when a woman entered the bus. Normally I would have just told her the bus had ended its journey but I decided to listen to her first. It turned out to be a general ticket-enquiry which ended in a happy conclusion. As she exited, I stepped off the bus to see if the car was still there. As I did, some bloke stepped on, walked up the back of the bus and sat down.

"Can I be of any assistance Sir?" I asked, knowing full well I couldn't. "City." came the reply; he hardly even looked in my direction. "Ah, could be a problem there Sir." suddenly I had his full attention. "This bus has finished for the night . . . (slight pause) this is its final destination." I wanted to add 'It precedes no more' in Monty Python 'this parrot is dead' type of voice. "What?" came the reply. Now did he mean Watt as in James Watt, the inventor of the second condensing-chamber on a steam engine or "What" as in Oh bugger. I suspected the latter.

"It is Sunday sir, with a reduced service and we bus drivers like to get a head start on sinning for bulk redemption next Sunday morning . . . Sir", entered my mind but remained unspoken. "Oh bollocks." he said and got off and so did I, only to find the blocked-in car had gone - I missed my chance to glare at them.

Just another day: Youth gets on bus
"London Road." in a monotone, says youth. Nice driver issues a single ticket and asks for money. Youth then informs driver "Child fare." Nice driver cancels ticket and issues a Single child fare ticket. Youth then informs driver "Return."
Nice driver cancels ticket and issues Return whilst sticking a pin in wax figure on dashboard.

Woman gets on bus, smiles at driver. Nice driver returns smile Woman remains smiling at driver. Nice driver starts to feel he's being visually mugged. Woman still smiling. Nice driver gives up and asks "Would you like to travel somewhere?", Woman realises she has to communicate orally.

Elderly woman gets on bus, shows driver her pass and asks "Can I use this to travel to the town?" Nice driver informs her that it would be better to use the bus as her pass doesn't seem to have any wheels.

Woman gets on bus with an American accent (it was in a box under her arm). Nice driver says "Lovely accent, where are you from?". "America." Woman replies. "Oh, what part?" asks driver. "All of me" replies woman.

Holding a Policeman's Helmet: 04:30 am. The day started like any other, the earth rotated 'round to face the sun, gravity remained in place – thankfully, and the elderly sat on the ends of their beds clutching their free passes waiting for nine o'clock.

Did I really have to get up at this time, oh yes, my bladder confirmed that it was important and I was on 'early starts'. Slipping out of my Thomas the Tank Engine PJ's and into the bathroom, I started my morning exercise . . . up down, up down, up down, then the other eyelid.

Friday marks the end of the week for most but not for bus drivers, it's just another day ending in 'Y'. The upside is, that I would be in the city before the rush-hour started and on my way back when it was nearly over. By 9:30, I'd be back in town for lunch/breakfast (now known as Lunchfast) and then repeat the same journey once more before clocking off at half past two.

The second journey proved to be the highlight of the day, for I was about to meet a punt and it was a good one. (Punt: the art of pushing a car out of a bus stop without physical contact)

The victim, or should I say 'ill advised driver', had parked in the middle of a busy bus stop, disregarding the free-space at each end. I drove in and lined up with the waiting passengers, which placed me nose to nose with the naughty car, but what was this I see?, a disabled badge, does this allow them to park in bus stops, no of course not, they get a little booklet telling them just where they can park and so they know better than most.

Passengers loaded, I beeped my horn. The car only had one occupant, the passenger. The driver was not present unless invisibility is a disability, however I suspected that it was the passenger that was disabled - she was of a rotund nature and had her own gravitational field.

Securing the bus, a brick on a length of string out of the window and a sign saying 'closed', I approached the car. "Is the driver around?" I asked, instantly regretting the word 'around' as in spherical. She jerked her head backwards, indicating the taxi office behind. Off I trotted to make further enquiries for said driver but found no joy.

Back on the street, I stood beside the car looking up and down the street. I was going to milk this for all of it's worth. As luck would have it, a police officer walked past completely oblivious of me, a badly-placed car and a great big bus that had now been blocked in behind by yet another illegally-parked car. "Officer," I called out, I had ensured a reasonable distance had been made between me and the policeman so I had to say it out loud and get everyone's attention. I had to say it twice before he stopped and turned.

I pointed to the car and the bus; he summed up the situation and approached the car. The passenger could offer no assistance as to the whereabouts of her spouse so he told her that he would move the car backwards to allow the bus to continue its journey, which she permitted. One problem arose here, for the nice policeman had a pointy helmet and the car had no sunroof to accommodate it and so he asked me to hold it for him.

Job done, I reluctantly handed back his helmet. I had mentally noted that his head didn't come to a point, boarded the bus, apologised to the passengers for the 'slight delay' and added "We won." They loved it, there's nothing like a bit of street theatre to entertain. The police officer informed me he would remain to speak to the driver. How I wished I could have stayed but at least I could brag to other drivers of holding a policeman's helmet and all the sexual innuendo that goes with it.

"I thought this was an 'every 10 minute' service" said the woman boarding the bus. "Yes." replied I, doing my best impression of someone who cared. "Well I've been waiting for half an hour now." she retorts. "I'm sorry, there has been a bit of a delay due to the road works on the seafront."

She didn't reply but offered up one of those looks that only women can - one of pure disbelief. Three stops later, we join the end of the traffic jam at said road works. 43 minutes later, we pass the obstruction - a journey that would normally take three minutes. She gets off and I offer up my usual "Thank you, have a lovely day." rather than the "I told you so." reply I wanted to give. Strangely, she didn't reply. Sometimes I get that warm feeling, like a burst colostomy bag.

Mother knows best: Did your mother ever say to you "Make sure you've got clean underwear on just in case you get run over by a bus." or is that just me? I guess the idea is, that whilst your laying there on in the emergency room at the hospital with pipes out of your nose, hooked up to a machine that just goes 'ping' every second, a nurse is cutting your trousers off with a pair of scissors and says "Oh doctor, try your best, he's wearing clean underwear." Somehow I know this won't be the case, not at that end.

Well, summer's here, a time when parking cones and roadworks blossom into life whilst the workmen, ever-wary of the nasty ultra-violet rays emitting from the big yellow thing in the sky, stay in the van, eating their sandwiches, waiting for the passing shadow of a cloud to wander out and crowd around the hole, pointing at nothing in particular.

One thing that did make me smile, happened about a week ago on a busy section of road. For some reason, they decided to re-seat the manhole covers on the bridge. Usual deal, single lane, temporary traffic lights and two very long lines of traffic and to pacify the road users, a yellow sign saying 'Delays possible, sorry for any inconvenience' which you only discover when you eventually reach the road works way too late to take avoiding action. One member of the road gang obviously had a sense of humour and a death wish too. He had placed a cardboard sign in front saying: The man in charge is Mick, his mobile number is *********.

I'm not one to speak ill of customers, my fingers were crossed when I wrote that, but today took the proverbial biscuit. Mum, dad, son, daughter and possible grandparent and I'm assuming a great deal here, boarded in the city and I took one look at them and the sound of Duelling banjo's filled the air. If you've not seen the film 'Deliverance', then 'squeal like a pig' will mean nothing to you, because 'Incest is a game the whole family can play'.

As drivers, we meet a lot of people who have problems - be they physical or mental and we rarely bat an eyelid but never had I met a family who were the spitting image of each other, were so loud and clapped every time the bus went round a corner. As for the other passengers, to a man, they spent the entire journey looking out of the windows in complete silence.

Embarrassing incident: A while ago, I had to run light to my start point and as is normal practice the sign on the front said 'Out Of Service', only because I lost my sign that said 'Leper bus'. Now of course, trundling down the road, people just see a bus, they want a bus, they don't care that one's not due or that no lights are on inside, they will stick out their hands, walking sticks or false limbs to catch my attention come what may. When we drive right past, they curse and complain. I'm often tempted to stop and explain but I know they will jump on or cling to the side of the bus, so on this one occasion I slowed down as I passed and pointed upwards at the sign saying Out Of Service above my head. It occurred to me that it would look very much like I was giving them 'The Finger', as our American cousins might say. From now on, I shall just sail past staring fixedly at the road ahead, which would make a change.

Brain . . . Manual not included: It's been an interesting week. Had a bit of a chat with a construction worker today in town, he had managed to park his van just off a mini roundabout where he had been working and was loading up his 'Men at work' sign when I came around the corner in my bus.

The problem was, I couldn't get between him and the traffic island without knocking down the Keep Left bollard. He took one look at me and said "You could get a bus thought there mate." whereas I replied "No I can't", "Yes you can, just keep it straight, it's simple" he answered back.

Now I certainly wouldn't presume to doubt his judgement when it came to digging holes in the road but it was a little annoying that he felt he knew better than I, the capabilities of driving a bus. I refused to move unless he was prepared to take full responsibility for the consequences. He declined this offer, loaded up his hire van and moved it forward, parking it directly over a pedestrian crossing. Some expert! The onlookers enjoyed it.

The other day, I was as happy as Larry; whatever the hell that's meant to mean. There was nothing left to ruin my day, until the last run back home. I boarded the passengers as normal; I'd left my silly hat at home. All were eager to get home, each had the right money (Bulls**t alert) and smiling (hitting the fan now) and we all sang a rousing chorus of Rule Britannia before we set off.

I had got no further than quarter of a mile, before the water alarm went off. I soon discovered that removing the bulb from the dashboard didn't stop the alarm, it was still shrieking. Hmm, reminds me of my honeymoon…I had to turn back to the bus station for a top up, and put some water in the bus too.

A chap from head-office was also travelling on the bus but he shall remain nameless (Hi Dave) and he reminded me to take caution when removing the water cap, it being pressurised, due to the boiling steam inside. At arms-length with a wad of paper between my hand and the filler cap, I slowly unscrewed it . . . Nothing, not a hiss or hint of steam.

We looked at each other and raised eyebrows in unison, which is a small town just north of London, in case you were wondering. Eyebrows still raised Roger Moore style, I poured in some of company's finest water, as passed by the management. It took less than a litre to fill to the brim. Our collective eyebrows were now on top of our heads - time for an expert opinion. Not having one at hand, we called for a mechanic.

I followed him around to the back of the bus, I had to, he was holding my hand. He opened up a side panel and uttered "hmm nothing wrong there" and closed it again. I then mentioned that it was actually the other bus behind us. He gave me a look (I still have it) and proceeded to prod about.

"How far you going?' he asked, "Back to town" I replied, "Oh . . . should be alright, run it back to town." What I think he meant, was that once it was past halfway, it was someone else's problem. By this time, we had transferred the passengers to another bus that had come in and thankfully, going the same way - possibly. We climbed back on-board and tentatively set off homeward bound, no reference to Simon and Garfunkel intended.

I'd like to say the trip was uneventful, in fact I will. The trip was uneventful, there, I've said it. The bus behaved moderately well, the alarm going on and off randomly, I dropped of the chap from head office (bye Dave) and carried on regardless until I got to an area known as the garden centre. From here, it's a short trip to town along the main 'A' road, or should have been. As I rounded the roundabout, the bastards had closed the town-bound exit.

It turned out they had chosen to install a footbridge across the road which no one will ever use. My diversion route would take me over 10 miles out of my way, in a bus that could boil dry at any moment. It was unfortunate I was running 'Out of Service'. Had I broken down with passengers, a spare bus would come out immediately to rescue them and me, leaving a mechanic behind with the crippled bus but as I was alone, I would be classed as 'non urgent' with a two hour wait for a mechanic somewhere out in the unfamiliar countryside, possible with those duelling banjo's. Oh, the problem with the bus, a short circuiting wire tripping the alarm.

"Thank you for waiting." said the elderly woman who had just run across the road in front of the bus as it pulled out, her arms rotating like a demonic windmill. "Well it was either that or run you over." I replied in my best having-a-joke-with-a-customer voice. "Where would you like to go?" I asked. "Oh anywhere." came the reply, Oh bugger thought I, one of those. "Where's your last stop driver?" she enquired? "The city"' I answered "Then the city will do." she finished.

She moved deeper into the bus, whilst rummaging through her handbag. This is a common ploy used by some older people, in the hope the driver will give up waiting and start the journey, eventually forgetting about them as time passes. I wasn't in the mood this morning because I knew there was entertainment value here for the rest of my customers.

"I'm afraid I can't move off until I issue a ticket ma'am." I called down the bus. She was at least a third of the way down the bus heading for a seat. She returned and handed over a plastic card to me. "I'm sorry." I said, "This is a library card." she took it back and produced another card, an AA car breakdown service card; I shuddered to think that she might just possibly own a car. "Sorry, this card is not the one.", "Oh, I shall have to sit down and look for it." she answered.

"I won't be able to move until I have some form of payment." I told her. "I'm almost 10 minutes late already, perhaps you would like to sit down on the bench in the bus stop and look for it, and another bus will be here in a few minutes.", I tried, as a last hope option whilst thinking I should have run her over in the beginning.

She returned and offered another card. Yes, you guessed it, a credit card. By now, the next bus was rounding the corner. "The next bus has turned up ma'am, I shall have to ask you to leave if you don't have means of payment," Yes, cruel I know but I can't carry anyone without a ticket, not worth risking my job for one little old lady. "Will this do driver?" she said, offering up a five pound note. "Yes, that would be perfect," I replied and issued a ticket with the thought in the back of my mind that she knew exactly what she was doing. She got off about halfway along the route.

Chapter seventeen: Trying it on.

The vermilion splash of blood on a freshly-formed elder leaf, the soft carpet of rabbit fur, ground into the black tarmac and the shades of grey on a pigeons wing waving in the breeze strangely absent from the rest of the body, the morning dew glistening from a dead badgers eye hanging from a twig on the roadside - all these wonders of nature only open to the early shift drivers. . . .

. . . An excerpt from Jimmy's next book: Jimmy and the Windmill of Doom. Published by Ginster Pie and Sausage Company, available as a hard-back with wipe-clean cover, coffee table version available soon, just as soon as we find some legs to fit it.

The bus stops halfway up a one-way street, a fire engine blocks the way. "What's that driver?" asks a woman passenger. "It's a fire engine." replies the driver. "What's it doing there?" says the woman, "Attending a fire." replies the driver, "Why have we stopped?" enquires the same woman. "There's a fire engine in the way." ends the driver in total disbelief.

None of this happened to me thankfully but to another driver, I am given to understand that they've not found her body yet!

Foreign students, you either love 'em or hate 'em. Me, I'll reserve my opinion for the moment. When it's a single student, then there's not really a problem but they tend to herd together like cattle and rush the bus the moment the door opens, snapping the legs of the elderly as they try to disembark.

I now stop short of the bus stop to give the more fragile a head-start to leave the bus and perhaps the opportunity to scrape the shins of the rushing students with their shopping trolleys. What does bug me, is that whilst they are here, they are under strict instructions to only speak English but this seems to have got lost in translation. They also think they can get away with certain tricks when it comes to fare-paying or using weekly passes. Surely, they must realise we know all the tricks in the book; this includes passing checked passes behind your back to your mate or dropping it out of the window to them.

A few days ago in the evening, I pulled into a nearby town a few minutes early. A small crowd were waiting for me. I frisk them as they board the bus, looking for knives, alcohol rub and illicit toffee-making machinery, when one gentleman decides to vent his spleen and tells all within hearing-distance, what a poor service the bus company was giving. I raised my eyebrow (I've had a small lever fitted in my pocket). "Is there a problem sir?" I asked, as I confiscated a knuckle-duster off an octogenarian. "Yes, we've been waiting here for 10 minutes and three buses stopped, put 'OUT OF SERVICE' up and drove off." he answered. "Ah, those would be ones that have finished their duties and were going back to the depot to be fuelled and cleaned sir." replied I. "Yes of course, you would say that wouldn't you." he answered back, in a disbelieving voice.

"It's quite true sir.", "Well why can't they carry passengers back, it's on the way, it's a total shambles.", "Unfortunately, once a service is finished they are no-longer insured to carry passengers.", "Sure." came his disbelieving reply.

What was annoying, is that in those 10 minutes he was waiting, no buses were due or time-tabled to arrive to carry passengers. The bus prior to me was on time, I was on time, in fact early, and the service was running as printed. Still, it's not as if he were paying for the service was he, he had a free pass. (Body still undiscovered at time of writing)

I'm a name, not a number: Yes, we have badges with our names on now and I always though my name was 'Oi you' - you live and learn. I have contemplated changing mine, the options being: Darling, The Artist Formally Known As Prince (too long), Mr H Shipman, Xyzyz (A Chinese national hero or Polish Politician - probably) or 'Yes I'm late – don't talk to me'.

Now there was that incident the other day. Lady got off the bus, I did stop, I'm considerate like that, and she wheeled her shopping trolley off the platform to the pavement below. I guess she had a lot of shopping in it, as the rim of one of the wheels parted company from the hub. I saw it happen, she didn't and waved me goodbye. I drove off with a smile (and the bus) wondering how she was going to get home on one wheel?

"You've got a trainee with you this morning" I was informed the other morning by Control. They smiled, I smiled back but mine wasn't real. Now we all have to start somewhere, I remembered those early days too well. "Can he drive?" I asked. This may sound a little strange but it has been known for the odd trainee to have no sense of direction and spend chunks of the day reversing a bus out of peoples driveways as in 'Turn right here . . . no, I meant where that road is not immediately into someone's garden.'

My concerns were unfounded however; he was keen, confident and a lot bigger than me.

I spent the first couple of rounds riding on the platform, which is like standing on the deck of a small boat, wearing roller skates and pretending you're in full control of your legs - knowing the passengers behind are watching and thinking "Why are there two drivers? Perhaps one's good at turning left and the other at turning right?"

The first trips were uneventful. By trip three, I was sitting behind him, not on the same seat I should add, just out of sight - it takes a bit of the pressure off him. I did shout out 'MY GOD WE'RE GOING TO CRASH' a couple of times but he was unfazed. Trip four found me halfway down the bus enjoying the ride, listening to the old ladies gossip which made me realise why I like it up front. It was then that it really dawned on me that I was a real Bus Driver.

Catching them out: The three old dears shuffled on to the bus. By 'dears' I mean elderly people, not as in venison. "Three to the city." said the elected spokesperson and held out her pass. Now it's easy enough to press the enter button three times, just an hours training, but I'm much wiser now and just press it once. The elected spokesperson gives me a strange look, she had it in her hand ready.

I looked over her shoulder and she clicked on, "Oh, he wants to see your passes girls." she said and low and behold, the passes were offered. "I'm sorry, that's an old pass, I can't accept it anymore." say I. "Well the other driver accepted it."

replied the elected spokesperson. "Tell me another one." replied I or rather wished I had but instead just paused. It was stand-off time. I got out a jigsaw puzzle. "How much is it?" the elected spokesperson eventually asked. "£3.70" I said, quick as a flash - as in a flash of light, not a dirty old man standing in an alleyway. "Oh, it was only £3.50 coming here." she said, this was her downfall.

If the other driver had accepted her free pass she wouldn't have paid to get here. I remained silent but my alter ego was running up and down the bus naked, try not to picture that please.

And there's more . . . I pulled in to the main bus stop in the middle of town, the crowd welcomed me in the usual fashion, waving, shouting, throwing rotten fruit etc. In the end, I had to open the doors and they heaved on, totally ignoring my handwritten sign saying 'Anthrax Quarantine Unit'.

As I dealt with people on an individual basis, I noticed three children being ushered on behind the paying passengers and noted the two mothers doing the ushering. After about a minute, these mothers boarded the bus at the back of the queue. "Two to Beacon Hill, please." she asked. I rang up the fares and added "Plus three children was it?" There was a pause, similar to one I had used earlier, except this one was yellow. "Yes." came the eventual reply - she thought I hadn't noticed the kiddies. I completed the tickets and told her the price. "What, I'm not paying that. We'll get a taxi, come on children, off the bus."

This did mean I had to cancel a string of tickets but it was worth every one. The strange thing was, 'round the corner, I was due to change drivers and have a break and so I wandered back into town to search the rubbish bins for food when I noticed the very same mothers back in the queue for the next bus. If I had had the time, I would have just stood in the bus stop in clear view and smiled at them.

We did a charity bus-pull along the sea front, OK, I didn't, I get out of breath taking my hands out of my pockets, and you know what, people still tried to get on. It proved so successful, the bus company has sold off the tow-truck.

One bus station has a new ruling for bus drivers reversing out of the bays - we have to beep the horns. Strangely, the public have a habit of walking across the forecourt behind revering buses. This gives rise at busy periods, to a cacophony of tuneless honking. On one occasion, everyone joined in and did a wonderful rendition of Beethoven's Piano Concerto number five, second movement - he had a gippy tummy that day. It brought tears to my eyes but I was peeling an onion at the time.

The past few months have been uneventful in the bus world that I call home, lots of moans and groans but not interesting reading, its easy to complain but hard to entertain. I've not crashed the bus for ages, nor have I run anyone over, they tend to dodge out of the way now, no-one's died in transit, but there's still time.

There was one amusing story I heard today, of a past incident. A driver was coming to the end of his round, when a customer who was getting off the bus, remarked to the driver that there was a wheelchair on-board, nothing unusual about that, you might think, except there was no-one in it and on-one else on the bus. It would seem this driver had the power to heal the lame; hopefully we won't nail him to a cross at Easter!

Chapter eighteen: The End of the road

This book had to come to an end eventually. Nothing new was happening, everything that happened had happened before, just different people in different places. I had hoped to end on a high note, a death.

I was hoping it would be one I wasn't responsible for - a natural one involving a passenger. Yes I know that sounds horrible but it happens and I wanted it to happen to me.

We get a lot of old people on the bus and I've had a couple of close calls. One concerned an old chap late one evening. He shuffled on with his walking stick and sat down within sight of my internal mirror, he was the only passenger. After a while, I noticed his eyes were closed - nothing to raise any concerns normally, except his walking stick fell to the ground with a loud clatter. Nothing . . . he didn't stir. A few moments later, it crossed my mind he might have snuffed it.

I felt a little awkward, I should stop the bus and go and find out, this would mean losing a minute of a forthcoming fag break - then I had a brainwave. I took a corner badly, making sure the rear wheels bumped up the kerb, jolting the bus. Magic, he came back to life!

The second occasion was much closer. Again, it was the evening as I pulled into a small seaside town, a passenger came up to me as they were leaving and drew my attention to an elderly couple seated behind the cab. I looked 'round to see that the woman was slumped in the seat; her husband besides her was gripping her sleeve trying to stop her sliding off the seat. Her eyes were closed.

They had got on in the town before, at a stop outside the local hospital, she was very frail I noted but he had been worse, he had two sticks and had a lot of difficulty walking, I remembered waiting for them to sit down.

I turned the engine off and approached the couple and crouched down in front of them. "I don't think your wife's very well sir." I said to him. I had to repeat it before I got his attention. "She'll be fine when I get her home." he said. He could hardly walk himself - how the hell he could possibly support her home? "I think she needs medical attention, she's definitely not well."

I had hoped that someone else would come up from the back of the bus to support me; just being there would have helped. The rest of the passengers remained unmoved in every sense of the word, except one young man who asked if we were going to be held up much longer. 'Bastard', I thought.

The old woman slumped further in the seat and I managed to ease her back a bit. I took her hand and told her husband that I think an ambulance would be best. I felt for a pulse, she had a thick coat on and I couldn't see if her chest was rising. I asked him her name and called it out to her, her eyes flickered open for a brief moment, at least I wasn't holding a dead persons hand. "Has she been ill lately?" I asked, knowing the person on the end of the phone would ask as I dialled 999. "She's just come out of hospital, she had an epileptic fit." I had a feeling it was her first and probably last. "Which service do you require?" asked the operator. "Ambulance please."

I answered as many questions asked by the ambulance call centre as I could while we waited for a crew to attend. It seemed like ages before I heard a distant siren getting louder but it was only a few minutes. I left the couple to wave it down, they weren't going anywhere.

The ambulance pulled up and I briefed the crew as they got on the bus. I got off and had a fag, knowing the next bus was due any moment. I flagged it down and transferred the passengers.

It was another 10 minutes before the crew took her off in a sort of wheelchair; the other crew-member helped her husband off. I caught the eye of the paramedic who very slightly shook his head. Did this mean she was dead or that she was dying? I really felt sorry for the couple. Old people can be a pain - most are lovely but the almost certain knowledge that the husband would be going home alone later was so very sad.

When I got home I told my wife I nearly got a stiffy on the bus! (Got to end on a funny note, haven't I?)

Bio:

James Henry was born in Surrey above a greengrocers shop owned by his father who he knew as 'Dad'. He has one elder brother Phillip who is the son of his mother or 'Mum'. James moved to the coast, aged one. He is married to his wife Karen and has three children, Cassandra, Alexandra and Phillipa. James is still currently a bus driver.

A witty and amusing look behind the scenes of becoming a bus driver. Follow Jimmy's journal journey from interview though medical, training and finally to a bus driver asking old ladies if buying a return ticket to the cemetery is really a good idea!

"An irreverent look at life in the bus lane." : A spokesman.
"So funny I nearly laughed twice." : Mr Twat.
"I'd buy it just for the title." : Jimmy the Bus Driver.
"He mentions 'bosoms' a couple of times." : A bus spotter.

3411036R00090

Printed in Great Britain
by Amazon.co.uk, Ltd.,
Marston Gate.